J. GRESHAM MACHEN

J. Gresham Machen

BY

Sean Michael Lucas

EP BOOKS

1st Floor Venture House, 6 Silver Court, Watchmead,
Welwyn Garden City, UK, AL7 1TS

www.epbooks.org
sales@epbooks.org

EP BOOKS are distributed in the USA by:
JPL Fulfillment
3741 Linden Avenue Southeast,
Grand Rapids, MI 49548.

E-mail: sales@jplfulfillment.com
Tel: 877.683.6935

First published 2015

ISBN: 978–1–78397–057–5

British Library Cataloguing in Publication Data available

Printed and bound in the UK by 4edge Limited

To the elders at
The First Presbyterian Church
Hattiesburg, Mississippi
With sincere gratitude
for your friendship and partnership
in the Gospel
Valiant-for-Faith All

CONTENTS

Timeline

professor of New Testament at Princeton Seminary

1917–19   Serves with the YMCA in France during World War I

1920   Attends his first PCUSA General Assembly

1921   Delivers Sprunt Lectures at Union Seminary in Virginia; publishes The Origin of Paul's Religion

1923   Publishes Christianity and Liberalism

1923–24   Serves as pulpit supply at First Presbyterian Church, Princeton, New Jersey

1924   The "Auburn Affirmation" published

1925   Publishes What is Faith?; the Special Commission of Fifteen appointed

1926   Elected by the board of directors to fill the chair of Apologetics at Princeton Seminary; General Assembly tables his election while committee on Princeton Seminary investigates

1927   Princeton Committee reports and is expanded to recommend a final solution to consolidating two-board structure at Princeton

1929   Commission recommends a single board of trustees; when two signers of the Auburn Affirmation are appointed

	to the board, Machen resigns and starts Westminster Theological Seminary in Philadelphia
1930	The Virgin Birth of Christ published
1932	The Hocking Report published as Re-Thinking Missions; Machen starts the Independent Board for Presbyterian Foreign Missions
1934	The "Mandate of 1934" issued by PCUSA General Assembly; directed at Machen and the Independent Board
1935	Machen tried for disobeying the "Mandate of 1934" and convicted
1936	The charges against Machen upheld by the PCUSA General Assembly; he leaves to start the Presbyterian Church of America (name changed to the Orthodox Presbyterian Church in 1939)
1937	Machen dies on January 1 in Bismarck, North Dakota

1

EARLY DAYS

When J. Gresham Machen died in 1937, one of the journalists who reflected on his death was the famed and often acerbic *Baltimore Sun* columnist, H. L. Mencken. No friend to orthodox Christianity, still Mencken viewed Machen as different from fellow fundamentalists like William Jennings Bryan and as more honest than the theological liberals who were pushing their agenda in the northern Presbyterian church. "Though I could not yield to his reasoning," Mencken noted, "I could at least admire his remarkable clarity and cogency as an apologist, allowing him his primary assumptions." This was far more respect than Mencken could give to Bryan: "Dr. Machen himself was to Bryan as the Matterhorn is to a wart. His Biblical studies had been wide and deep, and he was familiar with the almost interminable literature of the subject. Moreover, he was an adept theologian, and had a wealth of professional knowledge to support his ideas. Bryan could only bawl."

It was this respect that caused Mencken to dub Machen, "Doctor Fundamentalis."

The credit for Machen's wide and deep knowledge of the Bible and the Reformed faith belonged to his parents. When he was born on July 28, 1881, his father Arthur had just celebrated his fifty-fourth birthday, his mother Mary Gresham her thirty-second. They were a remarkable couple. A transplant from Washington, D. C. and Virginia by way of Harvard University, Arthur Machen became one of the leading lawyers in Maryland; his success brought about appointments, which he declined, as a judge of the Superior Court of Baltimore City and as a U. S. District Attorney. His son would later remember him as a tremendous reader, whose knowledge of languages included Latin, Greek, French, and Italian. And Arthur Machen's piety was profound, "a quiet stream whose waters ran deep." He served as a ruling elder for a number of years at Franklin Street Presbyterian Church in Baltimore.

As significant as his father's influence was, Machen's mother Mary (or Minnie as she was called) was more influential. She was an extraordinary woman: she published *The Bible in Browning* in 1903; she had a good grasp of botany and astronomy; and she was well read in a number of other areas. She was also a firm believer in the Presbyterian system of doctrine and was determined to impart it to her children. Machen later recalled that he learned the great truths of the Christian faith at home from his mother: "That was the best school of all; and in it, without any merit of my own, I will venture to say that I had acquired a better knowledge of the contents of the Bible at twelve years of age than is possessed by many theological students of the present day. The Shorter

Catechism was not omitted. I repeated it perfectly, questions and answers, at a very tender age; and the divine revelation of which it is so glorious a summary was stored up in my mind and heart."

And so, Machen's parents provided for his education as he grew up. He attended a private school, the University School for Boys run by W. S. Marston and located on Madison Avenue, just a few blocks from the Machen home on Monument Street. He received a thorough classical education with Latin and Greek at the core of his training along with Geometry, Algebra, Natural Science, English, and French. His family made sure that he took piano lessons and had exposure to the best literature.

But young Machen's real passion was sports—following them as a spectator as much as playing them. When he was a teenager, he was absorbed by baseball, especially the Baltimore Orioles of manager Ned Hanlon, which won three straight National League pennants from 1894 to 1896. When the league disbanded the Orioles, shifting many of their players to become the Brooklyn Dodgers, Machen's baseball fever ebbed for a time. He would become a huge college football fan, never missing the Princeton-Harvard game if he could help it. And he would develop an abiding love for tennis, one that would carry over to his days at Princeton and Westminster Seminaries.

Each summer until he was ten, the Machens spent several weeks in Macon, Georgia, with Minnie's Gresham family. The exposure both to the southern way of life and to the Greshams' extended relations—who included the poet Sidney Lanier—made an abiding impression on Machen. While later historians have over-emphasized Machen's "southernness," he clearly appreciated the hospitality and refinement that wealthy white people in the American South exhibited. Because these traits coincided with the lifestyle his family enjoyed in Baltimore, Machen's own self-understanding undoubtedly bore the marks of "southern gentility." After the Georgia Greshams passed away toward the end of the nineteenth century, the Machens took their vacations in the White Mountains in New Hampshire and eventually in Seal Harbor, Maine.

Machen entered the Johns Hopkins University as a seventeen-year-old undergraduate. Though the school continued to maintain its founding focus as a graduate institution, it did have an undergraduate program and the graduate faculty participated in that program. Machen did exceptionally well: in his first year, he won the Hopkins scholarship; he was honored as first in his class; and he was elected Phi Beta Kappa in 1901. However, he truly entered into the glories of Hopkins when he studied in the graduate seminar of the famous classicist Basil Gildersleeve. While Machen already knew Gildersleeve, who was his father's intimate friend for a number of years and a fellow church member at Franklin Street Presbyterian Church, he still cherished his graduate year with him: "In him," he noted, "was found a rare combination of accurate philological learning with something akin, at least, to literary genius." Machen excelled in the graduate program in classics and enjoyed the "Plato year" that focused on careful translation and discussion of passages from Plato's dialogues.

By 1902, Machen began to wrestle with what to do next. That summer, he took courses in banking and international law at the University of Chicago. He thought that perhaps he might study economics at Columbia University. Or maybe he would go on for further classics work. However, he began to reflect that training to become a classics professor or a philologist or a banker would not be ultimately satisfying. For some time, apparently, he had considered seminary as a way of combining his religious interests with his academic ones: "When the summer [of 1902] was over," Machen remembered, "I turned at last to the field upon which I had for some time been casting longing eyes. How much more worthwhile it is, if one is to apply modern scientific methods of research to ancient books, to apply them to those books whose every word is of an importance to humanity with which the importance even of Homer and Plato can never for one moment be compared!"

What made this decision for theological education surprising was that, while Machen later remembers "casting longing eyes" toward it for some time, at the time it appeared utterly spontaneous. As late as August 1902, he had written his parents that "the ministry I am afraid I can't think of" as a calling. And yet, clearly it had crossed his mind, more than once. After all, while at Hopkins, he had been very involved with the YMCA, serving on the executive council for the college's branch and attending association conferences at Northfield, Massachusetts, during three separate summer vacations. And he remained active and engaged in his home church, Franklin Street Presbyterian Church, during his college and graduate school years.

It was his home church pastor, Harris Kirk, who gave Machen guidance at the crucial time. In September, after "two splendid sermons" by Kirk, Machen was able to get thirty minutes with Kirk to confer about his future: "He encouraged me to go to Princeton Seminary, and seems to think that *if* I want to leave after a year, it will do no harm." Machen also received encouragement from Francis Patton, family friend and president of Princeton Seminary. As Machen wrestled with whether he should be at the seminary and whether he should enter the ministry, "with infinite patience [Patton] brought me through my doubts and helped me in my difficulties."

Thus, Machen enrolled as a student at Princeton Theological Seminary in the fall of 1902. The faculty of Princeton Seminary, now in its ninetieth year of existence, was at the height of its powers. William Park Armstrong, with whom Machen was immediately impressed, led the New Testament faculty. Machen was impressed because Armstrong used the same historical-critical-philological method that Gildersleeve used at Hopkins. Machen recalled that "no student in his classroom who knew anything whatever of modern methods of philological and historical research could help seeing that [Armstrong] was a modern university man of the very highest stripe." John Davis and Robert Dick Wilson, the latter of whom would later join Machen at Westminster Seminary, handled Old Testament. William Brenton Greene held the chair of Apologetics; when he retired in 1925, he wanted Machen to have that chair. Patton served as president and as professor of practical theology and John DeWitt was the professor of church history.

But the two stalwarts of the faculty were Geerhardus Vos and B. B. Warfield. Vos had joined the faculty as its first professor of biblical theology in 1892; and while his thick Dutch accent made his classroom lectures a bit ponderous, there was at least one time when he made an impact on

Machen. It was when Vos preached his sermon, "Rabboni," on Christ's appearance to Mary after the resurrection. "We had this morning one of the first expository sermons I ever heard. It was preached by Dr. Vos, professor of Biblical Theology in the Seminary," Machen wrote home. "He is usually rather too severely theological for Sunday morning. Today was nothing less than inspiring ... Dr. Vos differs from some theological professors in having a better-developed bump of reverence."

Warfield, though, would become Machen's favorite faculty member. To be sure, "when I was a student at Princeton I admired Warfield, as we all did; but I was far from understanding fully his greatness both as a scholar and as a thinker." It was only as he realized later how prodigious Warfield's scholarship had been—first as a New Testament exegete and textual critic, then as a systematic theologian and as a historian of dogma—that he began to understand fully his professor: "It may certainly be said, in general, that he had a truly encyclopedic mind." Later, as Machen came to understand the need for a thoroughly Reformed system of doctrine as the basis of a sound apologetic, he came to appreciate his former professor even more.

Machen continued to wrestle with his sense of calling throughout his first two years at Princeton. His letters home indicated a certain boredom or diffidence in his studies; he would later remember his "own immaturity when I was a student at Princeton" as evidence that "theological students are far from being so well qualified in the field of theological encyclopedia as they sometimes think they are." And yet, he clearly worked hard, especially in areas of interest. He won a New Testament prize at the end of his second year and was encouraged to go on for the Maitland Prize, which would fund a year of graduate studies abroad. He took additional courses in philosophy at Princeton University and attended university lectures by Woodrow Wilson and Henry Van Dyke. As a result, it may be that his public stance toward his parents was one of flippancy even as he struggled deeply over what he might do with his life.

Toward the end of his second year, in spring 1904, Patton recommended to Machen that he remain at the seminary after he finished his degree to teach New Testament Greek and related courses. In order to make preparations, Machen went to Germany during that summer in order to gain some acquaintance with the German language. Upon his return for his final year of seminary, he focused his attention on his classes and especially on his essay for the Maitland Prize. Not only did he win that prize and have his essay published in the *Princeton Theological Review*, but also the topic—"A Critical Discussion of the New Testament Account of the Virgin Birth of Jesus"—would serve as a long-time interest and would later result in a full-length monograph in 1930, *The Virgin Birth of Jesus*.

The main benefit of winning the Maitland Prize was the fellowship year abroad. Machen left for Germany in the summer of 1905, first to hike and enjoy the countryside and then to determine where he would focus his attention for New Testament studies. In the event, he ended up spending the winter term at Marburg University, where he was attracted by lectures by Adolph Julicher and Johannes Weiss, two leading German New Testament scholars. While at Marburg, Machen also attended theology lectures by Wilhelm Herrmann, the brilliant representative of nineteenth century German liberalism. As he later reflected on this time, Machen "always rejoiced greatly" that he had the privilege of hearing Hermann. "In one's contact with any great movement, it has always seemed to me important to attend to its best, and not merely to its worst representatives; and Herrmann certainly represented Ritschlianism at its best."

Indeed, Herrmann mesmerized Machen: "Only personal contact could reveal the contagious earnestness, the deep religious feeling, of the man. I felt, as I sat in that classroom, that it was the center of world-wide influence, a place from which a great current went forth, for good or ill, into the whole life of mankind." The personal piety of the theological lecturer made his intellectual solutions more palatable: the relegation to the realm of metaphysics of any questions about the historical reality of God, Jesus, Spirit, miracles, or salvation. These questions, Herrmann argued, could not be decided on the basis of historical work because such work would always be shifting, thus endangering the true religion of the heart. As one of Machen's biographers put it, "Herrmann made Liberalism wonderfully attractive and heart-gripping."

Herrmann's liberalism *was* attractive to Machen, as it was to Rudolf Bultmann, who was at Marburg at the same time, and as it would be to Karl Barth who would listen to Herrmann three years later. But more important were the questions that Herrmann raised: for Machen had been struggling for several years with aligning his intellectual commitments with a genuine piety based solidly on biblical data. While he came to see that Herrmann's answers were themselves intellectually specious, he also wondered whether critical New Testament scholarship could actually answer the deepest questions of his mind and heart. He listened with great interest to Julicher and Weiss, but also to Rudolf Knopf on New Testament Introduction and a young Walter Bauer on the Gospel of John. He went on to Gottingen for the summer term, where he continued to sample the best of this scholarship.

His time in Germany gave Machen one of the central problems of his New Testament scholarship and his broader apologetics: the relationship between faith and history. While conservative evangelicals in America may have been right on the matters of faith, they made a great mistake in dismissing the higher critics with a few words of summary condemnation. These higher critics were raising real questions about the historical basis of the Christian faith that had to be confronted if the faith was to be believed. On the other hand, these liberal critics gave unsatisfactory answers to the problem of faith and history because, like Herrmann, they relegated matters of faith to a metaphysical realm that could only be accessed by sentiment and intuition. In this regard, the liberal critics were just as anti-intellectual as conservative evangelicals; indeed, more so, because they rejected the historicity of the events and accounts of the biblical text itself.

The solution, as Machen came to see it, was to do historical work with the best tools that the modern world could offer in such a way as to demonstrate a firm basis for faith. And yet, it was at just this point that Machen struggled while in Germany: he was unsure whether the historical work would actually support the faith that he had been taught in childhood. Such was his intellectual honesty and integrity that he did not believe that he could teach in a theological seminary or serve as a minister if he did not hold to the faith once for all delivered to the saints.

By spring 1906, Machen was sure that he could not return to Princeton to teach New Testament and he regretfully told his mentor, Armstrong, that this was the case. However, Armstrong's reply gave Machen more time to consider the matter: "I want so much to have you come to Princeton and try this work of teaching for a year at least that my natural inclination would lead me to urge you to give the matter further and if possible favorable consideration. Yet my conscience tells me that I ought not to urge you to take a step for which you do not feel prepared. So I am going to leave the matter entirely in your hands." Such patience and evident good will and trust allowed Machen to pass by an opportunity to teach at Lafayette College.

In addition, Armstrong's patience also gave Machen space to think his way through how he might teach at Princeton even though he had not yet settled some of these conflicted issues of history and faith. A later letter from Armstrong assured Machen that he did not need to be licensed or ordained by a presbytery to teach at the seminary as an instructor. He further noted that "should you find after trying it that you could not teach in the Seminary because you had reached conclusions in your study which made it impossible for you to uphold its position you would simply say so" and would move on to something else.

When Machen returned to America at the end of the summer, he conferred with his family at Seal Harbor, Maine, and with Armstrong in Princeton. By the beginning of September, he determined to teach at Princeton for a year, with a clear understanding that he would return to Germany at the end of that time to prepare himself to become a teacher of classics. He still did not have confidence that this was the right decision; as Machen wrote his mother, "Nobody ever started a work with more misgivings—indeed with anything nearer despair of being able to carry the work through." In the event, Machen would remain at Princeton Seminary for twenty-three years.

2

HISTORY AND FAITH

The facts that Machen spent twenty-three years teaching New Testament at Princeton Seminary and that he became one of the most noteworthy defenders of Christian orthodoxy in the 1920s are surprising in the light of his intellectual struggles of 1905–06. While he did not settle his intellectual questions all at once, he soon came to find that he could answer those questions better at Princeton than Germany or Johns Hopkins or elsewhere.

Initially, Machen's relationship with William Park Armstrong was his "greatest delight." "Army" was thirty-two years old when Machen came to assist him in teaching New Testament. And his background bore similarities to Machen's own: born in Selma, Alabama, Armstrong was academically gifted, graduating from Princeton University when he was twenty and taking a Master of Arts degree from the college while he was studying at Princeton Seminary. After receiving his Bachelor of Divinity from the seminary, he was sent on a fellowship year to Germany, where he studied at Marburg, Berlin, and Erlangen. When he returned, he was made assistant to George Purves, who was then the incumbent of the New Testament chair. When Purves later returned to the pastorate, Armstrong was elected to the faculty.

With only seven years in age separating Armstrong and Machen, they were more like brothers or peers than mentor with pupil. That allowed Machen to wrestle with his doubts more openly, perhaps, than he might have done otherwise. As he later reflected, "One of Armstrong's strongest points is that he combines detailed knowledge of critical and historical questions with an understanding of great underlying principles. His wide reading in philosophy enables him to show the connection between schools of New Testament criticism and various schools of modern philosophy; but, above all, he is able to exhibit the connection between the supernaturalistic view of the New Testament and the theistic view of God and the world upon which the Christian religion depends." It was demonstrating these connections between history and faith that served as Armstrong's strong point, indeed that stood as Princeton Seminary's great contribution: "I think that this union between detailed scholarship and understanding of great principles was characteristic of the old Princeton Seminary," he noted. And because Armstrong, and Princeton, excelled in doing this, Machen was able to ask and answer his questions and doubts in relative safety.

Likewise, Machen's relationships with Francis Patton, who served as seminary president, and B. B. Warfield were significant as well. Machen revered his long-time family friend, Patton, in whom "the finest traditions of the institution were preserved." And in Warfield, Machen found an example of the kind of faculty member that he aspired to be. "What a wonderful man he was!" Machen remembered. "His learning was prodigious. No adequate notion of its breadth can be obtained even from his voluminous collected works." Even more important, though, was the way that Warfield "would go out of his way to give a word of encouragement to a younger man."

Thus, Machen's relationships with the faculty were instrumental as he started to answer the larger questions of history and faith that had caused such a crisis of faith while he was in Germany. Perhaps as important was the intellectual work of teaching. While he did have some advanced courses, Machen was the main instructor of elementary Greek for the first fifteen years of his teaching career. While he struggled to impart a reading knowledge of biblical Greek to his students, his time doing this reinforced in his mind the classical ideal for theological education.

In addition, Machen regularly taught the required course in exegesis, which invariably focused on Galatians. It was a letter that was particularly suited to Machen's concerns because it married key historical issues with significant theological concerns. As he worked with students through the historical issues of the Judaizers, the issues of Christian liberty, the relationship to Acts 15, and the theology of justification by faith alone, he found his own heart issues becoming settled. As one later student noted, "It felt not merely that Luther had been reborn, but that Paul himself had become alive, and was teaching and proclaiming as a fresh message the evangel that stands in irreconcilable opposition to 'another gospel which is not another.'" In those early years, though, teaching Galatians helped to reconcile Machen's head and heart.

What also helped Machen sort out the issues raised by his time in Germany was his early research and writing. That research focused on two major areas. One was continued work on Jesus' birth narratives in Luke's Gospel. Much of this work would be published in the *Princeton Theological Review* in 1912 and republished in *The Virgin Birth of Christ* in 1930. In these essays, Machen focused closely on textual issues: were the narratives original to Luke? Did they reflect a Palestinian or a Greek provenance? As such, were the narratives trustworthy historical artifacts? Of course, these historical questions had profound theological consequences—for if the birth narratives did offer trustworthy history, then they served as witnesses of Jesus' virgin birth and established the church's teaching. But in these initial articles, Machen only touched on the theological conclusions implicitly if at all.

The second area on which Machen focused was the relationship between Jesus and Paul. In a significant essay contributed to the faculty's published offering for the seminary's centennial celebration, Machen began to challenge the developing liberal consensus that the Apostle Paul represented "the second founder of Christianity" and that his contribution was to move Christianity toward dogmatism and away from the simple ethical religion represented by Jesus. Machen noted that Paul did not view himself that way, but rather saw himself as part of the larger apostolic witness to Jesus, his teaching, and especially his death and resurrection.

But the way Machen made his larger case in response

to liberalism was genius and drew from his teaching of Galatians in his New Testament exegesis courses: he focused on Paul's interactions with the Judaizers, the "conservative" group that held on to the Jewishness of this new faith that came from Jesus. At each point, Machen observed, the apostles sided with Paul against the Judaizers: on the matter of Christian freedom; on the nature of justification by faith alone; on the person of Jesus as the Son of God and the "exalted Christology" in Colossians 1. Far from establishing a starkly different version of the faith than that intended by Jesus, Paul presented a faith that cohered with the rest of the apostolic band as demonstrated through his conflicts with the Judaizers. Machen would continue over the next decade to work on the significance of Paul and his relationship to Jesus.

These two intellectual tracks—the virgin birth of Jesus and the origin of Paul's religion—not only dealt with key theological issues for the Christian faith. They also served as examples of the deeper issue with which Machen continued to wrestle: the relationship between history and faith. By 1913, he had largely worked his way through those issues; and the fruit of his wrestling came in the form of two addresses that were later published in the *Princeton Theological Review.*

The first, "Christianity and Culture," was given at the opening of the seminary's 1912–13 school year and was published in early 1913. For those who knew about Machen's conflict over his calling and whether even to come to teach at Princeton in 1906, the opening paragraph and thesis had to sound familiar: "Some men have devoted themselves chiefly to the task of forming right conceptions as to Christianity and its foundations. To them no fact, however trivial, has appeared worthy of neglect; by them truth has been cherished for its own sake, without immediate reference to practical consequences." Here was a clear reference to Machen's own perspective: the scientific or academic tendency. And yet there was an admission about how difficult such a tendency was when it came to Christianity: "The scholar must apparently assume the attitude of an impartial observer—an attitude which seems absolutely impossible to the pious Christian laying hold upon Jesus as the only Savior from sin." And so, the question becomes how to maintain a scientific tendency and a simple faith in Jesus, how to hold together "culture" and "Christianity."

There were three potential solutions to how to do this. One was to subordinate Christianity to culture. This involved denuding Christianity of anything "supernatural" so that religion becomes a human product. Another was to "destroy culture," by making intellectual labor and the world itself "a matter at least of indifference to the Christian." The final and best solution was consecration. "Instead of destroying the arts and sciences or being indifferent to them, let us cultivate them with all the enthusiasm of the veriest humanist, but at the same time consecrate them to the service of our God," Machen declared.

For those who consecrate their intellectual labors to God's service, what they find is that they enter into their labors right at the point of the culture's deepest need. In the current day, the historical questions about Christianity's truthfulness had to be answered. This was a place where the Christian could use his consecrated labors in order to bring every thought into subjection to Jesus. And yet that was the case with every human endeavor. In a passage that echoed nineteenth-century theologian Abraham Kuyper, Machen declared, "The Christian cannot be satisfied so long as any human activity is either opposed to Christianity or out of all connection with Christianity. Christianity must pervade not merely all nations, but also all of human thought. The Christian, therefore, cannot be indifferent to any branch of earnest human endeavor. It must all be brought into *some* relation to the gospel." Here was a mandate to claim every area of life for Christ. Only if Christians did so and took up the intellectual challenge of the times would they reach their generation with the gospel of Jesus.

Machen's address was a clear note that he had resolved his intellectual crisis on the side of the Christian faith. Another signal was his willingness to go through the ordination process and so become a Presbyterian minister. By November 1913, Machen came under the care of a presbytery; he was licensed to preach the Gospel in April 1914, elected assistant professor of New Testament the next month, and ordained as a minister in June 1914. A process that had started in 1902 when he first came to Princeton Seminary came to completion.

A final signal that he had resolved the inner conflict was his second major address, which he gave as part of his installation to his professorship in May 1915. Entitled "History and Faith," Machen started with several straightforward propositions: "The student of the New Testament should be primarily a historian. The center and core of all the Bible is history. Everything else that the Bible contains is fitted into a historical framework and leads up to a historical climax. The Bible is primarily a record of events." From there, Machen defended these propositions against various forms of theological liberalism that all boil down to the same idea, namely that "the true essence of the Bible is to be found in eternal ideas; history is merely the form in which those ideas are expressed."

However, if history were merely the form in which the eternal ideas were expressed, then the result would be to cut off Christianity from history. And that would make Christianity a failure—because at the heart of Christianity was the gospel, a statement about good news. "In other words, it means history. A gospel independent of history is simply a contradiction in terms," Machen claimed. But the gospel was rooted in history because it was news; it was about something that had happened and especially something that had happened about Jesus.

That meant the Christian faith had everything to do with history and historical investigation. Central to that historical investigation was whether the Bible was right about Jesus. How would the historian attack that issue? He started with some of the earliest documents, the writings of Paul. What the historian found in Paul's letters was faith in Jesus as God and knowledge about Jesus as man; witness to his crucifixion as an atoning sacrifice and to his resurrection as both bodily and securing vindication before God. And yet, these opinions were not restricted to Paul alone; all of Jesus' disciples held the same.

When one considered the Gospels, one would find that the picture of Jesus given there agreed with Paul's letters. All four Gospels viewed Jesus as a divine person and as a human person. All four highlighted the crucifixion and the resurrection. All four noted that Jesus was a supernatural person who had the power to do mighty deeds and the authority to say mighty words. These Gospel writers agreed with Paul—the news that they report has to do with Jesus as a real historical person who was divine and human and who died and was raised.

Though the liberal tried to separate the divine from the human in the Gospel accounts by "demythologizing" them, such an attempt was a failure. "Such separation is impossible," Machen declared, "Divine and human are too closely interwoven—reject the divine, and you must reject the human too." The liberal tried to do this, only to end up with a Jesus who stands as a "monstrosity." The ethical Jesus of the liberal could never have made the claims that the Gospel writers reported. He would never have claimed to be the Son of God or the judge of the world as Jesus does. The only solution for those sayings was to claim that they were inauthentic, with the result that the Bible actually offered very little of what Jesus said and did. But all of this was a failure: "the modern substitute for the Jesus of the Bible has been tried and found wanting."

When Jesus was examined historically, what one discovered was that the Bible "is right at the central point; it is right in its account of Jesus; it has validated its principal claim." Faith and history were reconciled through a careful consideration of the Bible and its claims: "The Bible is at the foundation of the church. Undermine that foundation, and the church will fall. It will fall, and great will be the fall of it." All in all, Machen's inaugural address was a *tour de force* that signaled the end of his doubts about the truthfulness of Christianity or its importance for his own life.

It also signaled his continued concern about the relationship between Jesus and Paul. He would continue to work on this theme for the next several years, eventually producing his first monograph, *The Origin of Paul's Religion*, in 1921. Undoubtedly, the book would have appeared sooner if World War I had not intervened and if Machen had not decided to serve in Europe with the YMCA. That he did in fact serve was a bit surprising, especially in the light of his pro-German sympathies leading up to 1917 and his lack of enthusiasm for American participation in a largely European squabble.

And yet, serve he did. The primary reason Machen volunteered to assist the war effort was his own intense patriotism. All through the lead-up to America's entrance into the war, he had expressed concern that American ideals were threatened by British imperialism and German pretentions. And when the United States Congress proposed permanent compulsory military service, he protested on the grounds that such a proposal threatened "Americanism," by which he meant "American liberty and the whole American ideal of life." He was keen to see America preserved and strong in the midst of the world crisis.

As a result, by August 1917, Machen had decided to serve the war effort through the YMCA. Throughout the fall, he was occupied in preaching at various stateside military camps under YMCA auspices. He was gone almost every Sunday, preaching to the men who were preparing to head off to France to fight in the war to end all wars. Toward the end of 1917, he sustained the physical exams necessary for his own departure to Europe and by the end of January

1918, Machen arrived at Bordeaux, France, for over a year's worth of service with the YMCA.

Most of Machen's work occurred around Soissons, which was a little more than sixty miles to the northeast of Paris. But he did move around a bit: as he later told his mother, "To sum up, I saw something of five sectors of the front—Aisne, Lorraine, Argonne, Woevre, and Belgium." His main work was to maintain a "Y" canteen hut, which not only served as a library with around 200 books for the soldiers' use, but also functioned as a commissary, selling various snacks, toiletries, and other necessaries. And while he had one near scrape with the Germans, on the whole Machen stayed out of harm's way.

However, he was unable to do the kind of preaching to the soldiers that he had hoped to do. Instead he was forced to continue to do the canteen work because there were so few YMCA secretaries when compared to the number of American soldiers on the ground in France. That reality, coupled with the struggle to get supplies necessary for the canteen work to progress, meant that Machen was exhausted much of the time and frustrated by his lack of ministry opportunities.

When the armistice was declared, Machen rejoiced: "Hardly before have I known what true thanksgiving is … It seems as though the hills must break forth into singing. Peace at last, and praise to God!" The end of the war did not mean that Machen returned to America immediately, however. In fact, it was once the war was ended that Machen had opportunities to preach the gospel to troops as they were returning home. From November 1918 to February 1919, Machen preached regularly in the camps and found a frequent sense of divine blessing upon his ministry. By the beginning of March, he was finally on his way home to America.

What a different country he would find upon his return. Though only gone fifteen months, Machen would find that his return to his country and his seminary work would plunge him into a new kind of war: a battle to maintain the faith once delivered to the saints. At some level, it was a continuation of the internal struggle that he had faced in sorting out the relationship between history and faith: was the Jesus of the Bible to be trusted as a historical person? And if so, then what difference did that make for life in the world today?

Already Machen was raising these questions and their implications for the church. In a chapel address at Princeton Seminary two months after he had come home, he suggested that the church had failed to connect with the men who had fought in the recent war. "If the church has failed," he observed, "It is at least perfectly clear why she has failed. She has failed because men have been unwilling to receive, and the church has been unwilling to preach, the gospel of Christ crucified." Instead, the church preached "muscular Christianity"—the value of self-sacrifice, the nobility of service—instead of biblical Christianity. "Men have lost sight of the majesty of Jesus' person" and have instead embraced a form of paganism that went forth under the name of Christianity: a view of life that found its ideal in "a healthy and harmonious and joyous development of existing human facilities." That was the exact opposite of Christianity, which proclaimed to men that they were sinners in need of a Savior.

This kind of full-throated Christianity was absent from the popular Protestant pulpits and the scholarly world to which Machen had returned. In response, he continued to provide a historical defense of the gospel through his work on Jesus and Paul. He shared that work in the Sprunt Lectures at Union Theological Seminary in Virginia in 1921, which would find a fuller form in the soon-published *The Origin of Paul's Religion*. The issues were the same as the ones he raised in 1912: was Paul the founder of Christianity? Or was he simply the conveyer of an apostolic tradition that had its roots in Jesus himself?

Machen deployed all his scholarly arguments to show that Protestant liberalism offered no compelling arguments to overturn the traditional understanding that Paul was a transmitter of a prior Jesus tradition that had its roots in historical facts about Jesus himself. He would soon find the need to recycle these academic perspectives for a more popular audience within his own Presbyterian church and he would be surprised to be identified as a "fundamentalist" for doing so. Such was the price to pay to defend the faith and to remain true to the historical facts represented by the Bible itself.

3

CHRISTIANITY AND LIBERALISM

It is somewhat surprising that Machen became associated in the popular mind with Protestant fundamentalism. After all, so much of his struggle as a graduate student over the problems of faith and history—and the answers he came to—appear far away from the popular image of fundamentalists fostered by H. L. Mencken's caricatures of them as uncultured barbarians who clung to outmoded religion. And yet, both during the 1920s and long afterward, Machen was viewed as a defender of fundamentalist Christianity, albeit of the "scholarly" type.

To be fair, while Machen disliked the term "fundamentalist," he willingly identified with it when contrasted with theological liberalism or "modernism." He probably was a forerunner of a later generation's "evangelicals," both in terms of his scholarly approach and in terms of his adherence to a more mainstream version of Protestantism. As he would note in 1924, "The term 'fundamentalism' ... is evidently to be taken in a broad sense, not to designate 'Premillennialists' but to include all those who definitely and polemically maintain a belief in supernatural Christianity as over against the Modernism of the present day." Whenever Machen addressed these issues for a public audience, he made common cause with Protestant fundamentalism because he saw that movement as defending "the historic Christian faith."

However, his real interest was in maintaining the historic Christian faith as expressed within his own Presbyterian church. He was certainly aware that there were moves being made within his communion toward the theological liberalism that had appealed to him while studying at Marburg. Two sets of events occurring around 1920 served to highlight how far theological liberalism had made its way into his beloved communion and threatened the faith once delivered to the saints.

The first was connected to the burgeoning ecumenical movement. At the end of World War I, various forces within the mainstream Protestant denominations in the American north began to work towards organic union. While the rhetoric for church union emphasized a sentimentalized unity that could overcome all human ills and preserve western civilization, the theological underpinnings were far more problematic. Not only were denominational distinctives jettisoned in order to forge potential unity, but also understandings of core Christian doctrines were broadened in order to include a range of beliefs.

Machen was undoubtedly aware of the movement within

Presbyterian circles toward church union because his seminary's president, J. Ross Stevenson, as well as his seminary colleague, Charles Erdman, were involved on the Presbyterian Church in the United States of America (PCUSA) Committee on Church Cooperation and Union from its inception in 1918. But with the report of this committee at the 1920 General Assembly, to which Machen was sent as a commissioner, the doctrinal basis of the proposed church union came clear.

In response, Machen published three articles in *The Presbyterian* against the proposed plan of union. In the first article, he attacked the doctrinal preamble of the plan. The opening statement had detailed the "shared beliefs" of the cooperating denominations that would serve as a basis for church union; however, the preamble actually had omitted "all the great essentials of the Christian faith." Along this line, the doctrinal statements of the particular uniting churches were treated as "purely denominational affairs." And yet, for Presbyterians, the Westminster Standards could never be regarded this way: "those who believe it to be true will never be satisfied until it has been accepted by the whole world, and will never consent to be limited in the propagation of it by any church or union of churches whatsoever."

Machen extended this line of opposition in his next two articles. The failure of the plan of union to take doctrinal matters seriously meant that the union was "committed to a denial of the Christian faith." In fact, the preamble was a "manifesto of that naturalistic liberalism which is the chief enemy of Christianity in the modern world." As such, it was "anti-Christian to the core." While some might be willing to unite with a conglomerated church that represented "a unity of organization which covers a radical diversity of aim," Presbyterians who take their doctrinal standards seriously should oppose such union.

In the event, although the drive for church union succeeded in Canada, it failed in the northern United States. That did not mean, however, that Machen's concern abated. As he began to connect the dots between the questions of history and faith with which he had been concerned in his academic work and the denial of doctrinal truth evidence in the plan of union, he began to raise even more questions about whether the northern Presbyterian church could hold together long-term.

A second event crystalized Machen's concerns about his church: the ministry of Harry Emerson Fosdick at First Presbyterian Church, New York. A Baptist preacher, Fosdick was a professor at Union Theological Seminary in New York while supplying the pulpit of First Church. Well-known as a winsome voice for Protestant liberalism, Fosdick attracted little attention from conservative Presbyterians until he preached his combative sermon, "Shall the Fundamentalists Win?"

Preached on Sunday morning, May 21, 1922, Fosdick's sermon was a broadside against coalescing northern Baptist and Presbyterian fundamentalism. He not only attacked core doctrines of historical Christianity, but he raised a more troubling question, "Has anybody a right to deny the Christian name to those who differ with him on such points and to shut against them the doors of the Christian fellowship?" Fundamentalists argued that such boundaries must be maintained; Fosdick and other Protestant liberals said that no one could make those determinations and so all those who call themselves Christians should be honored as such, even if they deny the supernatural elements of the Bible.

Two factors made Fosdick's arguments troubling. The first was that they were made from the pulpit of a Presbyterian church; the other was that it appeared that there were a number of Presbyterians who agreed with him that a diversity of opinion on historic Christian doctrines should be allowed. While that may not have been problematic for Baptists, who generally refused to subscribe to a creed, it was deeply troubling for Presbyterians, who required their ministers to subscribe to the Westminster Standards. What did such liberality in doctrinal commitment mean in a connectional and confessional church like the Presbyterian Church in the USA?

For Machen, these two issues—the ecumenical movement with its denigrating of Presbyterian doctrinal particularities and the allowance of Fosdick's ministry in a Presbyterian pulpit—propelled him to raise his voice on behalf of "fundamental" Christianity within his church. Machen first aired his developing concerns a few months before Fosdick's sermon, in a November 1921 address to a conference of ruling elders in Chester Presbytery, meeting just outside Philadelphia. The conference had assigned him the topic, "the present attack against the fundamentals of our Christian faith, from the point of view of colleges and seminaries." His response was formed in terms similar to his objection to the ecumenical plan of union: the attack against the fundamentals of the faith "may all be subsumed under the general head of 'naturalism'—that is, the denial of any entrance of creative power of God (in distinction from the ordinary course of nature) in connection with the origin of Christianity." This naturalism was at the heart of "liberal" religion, even though liberal Christianity denied having any specific teachings. Rather, according to liberalism, what was truly important was experience of the divine, not teaching about the divine; what was important was life, not doctrine.

Against this, Machen argued that if one went back to the very origins of Christianity, one would understand that the apostolic generation did not view their faith in these terms. Instead, the first generation of Christians was very concerned about historical facts and the meaning of those facts: Jesus Christ died, was buried, and rose again according to the Scripture. And he did so, not for himself, but for others. Historically speaking, Machen contended, "Christianity is based upon an account of something that happened." To deny this in place of a sentimental, universal experience of the divine was to move from Christianity to liberalism.

This basic argument, first made before ruling elders in northwest Philadelphia, would be the framework of Machen's extended critique of liberalism in his book *Christianity and Liberalism* (1923). Machen took as his starting point the same question that Protestant liberals were asking: could Christianity be maintained in "a scientific age"? Theological liberals believed that Christianity could only be maintained in the face of "new science" if it adapted to the naturalism of modern science or if it were separated from scientific investigation entirely. The former solution involved a series of concessions by religion to naturalism that would result in an entirely different religion from Christianity. The latter claim, that "religion is so entirely separate from science, that the two, rightly defined, cannot possibly come into conflict," expressed a profound skepticism toward knowledge in general. In other words, Protestant liberalism failed because it was unchristian and because it was unscientific. In *Christianity and Liberalism*, Machen would pursue the argument that liberalism was unchristian; in his book *What is Faith?* (1925), he would take up the other line, that liberalism was unscientific or anti-intellectual.

In order to demonstrate the first line of argument—theological liberalism was unchristian—Machen arraigned liberalism against the standard of Christian orthodoxy, summarized in all of its great creeds and especially, for his mainly Presbyterian audience, in the Westminster Standards. As the historian D. G. Hart rightly noted, *Christianity and Liberalism* reads more like a primer in Christian theology, less like a piece of theological polemic. The key difference between theological modernism and historic Christianity was that historic Christianity asserted the logical priority of doctrine over experience.

Again and again, Machen stressed this point: the Christian movement at its inception was "based, not upon mere feeling, not upon a mere program of work, but upon an account of facts. In other words, it was based upon doctrine." Doctrine was not simply the second order arrangement that later theologians foisted upon the experience of the founding generation; rather, "from the beginning, the meaning of the happening was set forth; and when the meaning of the happening was set forth then there was Christian doctrine. 'Christ died'—that is history; 'Christ died for our sins'—that is doctrine. Without these two elements, joined in an absolutely indissoluble union, there is no Christianity." To deny this doctrinal basis of Christianity was to place oneself against Christianity itself.

If the Protestant liberals were successful in doing away with doctrine, they would do away with "the very heart of the New Testament." They were not doing away with doctrinal statements from past ages like the seventeenth century or the great creeds of the early church; rather, they were standing "against the Bible and against Jesus himself." Here then was the great difference between Christianity and liberalism: liberalism promoted "life," while Christianity proclaimed a message; liberalism held forth an unhistorical experience, Christianity taught historically grounded doctrine.

In the rest of *Christianity and Liberalism*, Machen arraigned theological liberals' views on major doctrines— God, humanity, the Bible, Christ, and salvation—and contrasted them with historic Christianity. In his telling, liberalism presented a God who was one with the world process, a God who was solely immanent; Christianity worshipped God transcendent. Liberalism offered "supreme confidence in human goodness"; Christianity declared the reality of sinful human nature. Liberalism affirmed Christian experience as its sole authority; Christianity defended the authority of the inerrant Scriptures. Liberalism esteemed Jesus as an example of man's faith in God; Christianity worshipped Jesus, the God-man, the object of faith. Liberalism presented the atonement as the great example of self-sacrifice; Christianity held forth the atonement as an one-time substitutionary sacrifice for sin and the only way of salvation.

As a result of the vast difference between naturalistic modernism and supernatural Christianity, Machen believed that it was inconceivable that the two religions should abide in the same institution. "A separation between the two parties in the Church," he proclaimed, "is the crying need of the hour." And if liberalism and Christianity should not exist within the same denomination, they certainly should not coexist in a united church like that proposed by the plan on church union. Those who advocated church union on a minimalistic creed not only set aside doctrines that evangelical Protestants held to be true, but also they promoted a dishonest program. It was dishonest because evangelical Protestants believed that their creeds and doctrinal statements were true and established parts of their church's constitutions. To be paid by a congregation or institution that ostensibly required the upholding of doctrinal and constitutional positions only to wage war against those same positions represented a dishonest use of funds given by well-meaning and trusting laypeople. As a result, theological liberals in each denomination should abandon their churches and institutions and form their own liberal denomination. That would be the honest and right thing to do, leaving behind the churches and institutions to those who intended to uphold the denomination's doctrinal position.

The response to Machen's *Christianity and Liberalism* was, perhaps, predictable. Evangelical Protestants across denominational lines hailed the book as a scholarly dissection of liberalism. From liberal Protestants, the reaction was more negative. Typical was the response of Gerald Birney Smith, claiming that "the main impression gained from a reading of the book is its futility ... The book is an admirable illustration of the futility of attempting to deal with the development of Christianity in Protestantism by the methods employed by the Church of Rome." Strong-armed arguments would not turn anyone back to the "individualistic," authoritarian Christianity that Machen represented.

A more telling response was the arguments that liberal Protestants offered over the next several months. By 1924, two notable Protestant liberal scholars had authored books that set forth their version of Christianity in more positive form: William Merrill's *Liberal Christianity* and Shailer Mathews's *The Faith of Modernism*. Merrill, the long-time pastor of the Brick Presbyterian Church, New York City, set forward the perspective of a liberal Presbyterian, suggesting that Christianity was fundamentally a "personal relationship with the Father through Christ" that produced "pure, loving personal relationships." Echoing the philosophical personalism of Borden Parker Bowne, Merrill ironically confirmed Machen's claim that liberal Christianity privileged experience over everything else including doctrine. Mathews, academic dean at Chicago Divinity School, also agreed with Machen in a sense, proclaiming that "modernism" was not a set of doctrines as much as it was an attitude: "if the temptation of the dogmatic mind is toward inflexible formula, that of the Modernist is toward indifference in formula." And yet, there was some "doctrinal" center for liberalism: it was a confidence that "good will, though never fully realized, is of the nature of God, and is the law of progress." Human beings were fundamentally good; God's Spirit was present in all humans of good will; what was required was to move forward with the "example of Jesus" in order to work and do his good pleasure. Machen's observation that liberalism was not Christianity was unwittingly confirmed, not denied, by two of its defenders.

This doctrinal indifferentism and experiential moralism represented by Merrill and Mathews became codified for northern Presbyterians by early 1924 in the "Auburn Affirmation." In August 1923, Robert Hasting Nichols, a professor at Auburn Theological Seminary, Auburn, New York, had gathered likeminded folks together to discuss how to respond to Machen's defense of orthodoxy. He settled on preparing a statement that defended the freedom of liberal Presbyterian ministers to teach other interpretations of doctrines such as "the inspiration of the Bible, the Incarnation, the Atonement, the Resurrection, and the continuing life and supernatural power of our Lord Jesus Christ." The Auburn Affirmation was released on January 9, 1924, and caused quite a stir in the church. Appended to the document were the signatures of 150 Presbyterian ministers; eventually almost 1300 ministers and elders would sign the affirmation.

Machen was able to send a statement to the *New York Times* that was published beside the Affirmation. He suggested that "the declaration as a whole is a deplorable attempt to obscure the issue." But, in fact, the document demonstrated the accuracy of Machen's analysis: "The plain fact is that two mutually exclusive religions are being proclaimed in the pulpits of the Presbyterian Church." On the one side was historic Christianity that affirmed the traditional understanding of the doctrines about which the Affirmationists wrote; on the other side was Protestant liberalism, which denied the supernaturalism required by the Bible's teaching on these matters.

Later, Machen wrote a counter-affirmation, which was not circulated widely. In the document, Machen claimed that the Auburn Affirmation "advocates the destruction of the confessional witness of the Church" by interpreting doctrines in ways at variance to the "plain sense" of the Westminster Standards. Whereas the Affirmationists claimed that unity would be fostered by doctrinal pluralism, Machen believed that unity could be maintained "only by maintenance of the corporate witness of the church. The church is founded not upon agnosticism but upon a common adherence to the truth of the gospel as set forth in the confession of faith on the basis of the Scriptures." The only unity the church could know was a common adherence to doctrinal particularity.

Throughout this period, Machen was active in making his case to American Protestants generally and to the Presbyterian church particularly. While he refused to join conservative organizations that required doctrinal tests on secondary issues such as dispensational premillennialism, he repeatedly accepted invitations that allowed him to work with conservative co-belligerents across denominational lines who were concerned about the strength of Protestant liberalism. Not only did he preach regularly at First Presbyterian Church in Princeton, New Jersey, but he also accepted invitations to Union College; the Methodist ministers of the Camden, New Jersey, district; the Marble Collegiate Church under the sponsorship of the National Bible Institute; the Philadelphia Ministers' Association; the YMCA in Easton, Pennsylvania, along with students from nearby Lafayette College; Founders' Week at Moody Bible Institute; a Baptist conference in Philadelphia; the Pennsylvania State YMCA

Convention; and a Union Bible Conference sponsored by Moody Bible Institute. One reason to note Machen's itinerary is to raise the point: while Machen had a primary focus on his own Presbyterian church, he saw himself as a Presbyterian evangelical and an evangelical Presbyterian. He knew that the fight for historic Christianity required linking arms not just with evangelicals within the Presbyterian church, but across denominational lines.

In the end, however, Machen saw himself primarily as a Presbyterian, one who delighted in his church's confessionalism. Of course, he believed that the confessionalism of the Presbyterian tradition represented orthodox Christianity in its purest form. But that belief did not make him sectarian. Instead, it gave him a basis from which he could enjoy Christian fellowship and participate in Christian ministry across denominational lines with those who affirmed Christian orthodoxy. He would continue to welcome all those to join with him in the defense of the faith, even as he would eventually work towards a true Presbyterian church, not an interdenominational association, fellowship, or network.

4

FIGHTING THE GOOD FIGHT

While Machen welcomed all comers in the fight against theological liberalism, he also recognized that some approaches to the defense of the faith were better than others. His own approach, which refused to give ground on the central matters of faith and history, fact and doctrine, meant that sometimes he was out of step with other evangelicals who offered different approaches. Defenses of the faith that prioritized religious experience as the sole or even primary apologetic for the Christian faith or those that recast doctrines in the light of modern philosophical categories were traveling down a pathway that would actually betray the defended faith in the end, he believed. Likewise, those who became distracted by debates over creation or the end times were ultimately missing the central issue facing the Protestant church, namely, the person and work of Jesus. And so, as the middle years of the 1920s unfolded, Machen carefully distinguished his own robust approach from other less helpful evangelical apologetic methods.

One exchange that demonstrated significant differences between Machen and other evangelical theologians was with E. Y. Mullins, the longtime president of the Southern Baptist Theological Seminary. A contributor to the collection *The Fundamentals*, Mullins was as concerned about the theological drift experienced in American Protestantism as Machen. Starting in 1923, Mullins began raising questions about the "present situation in theology" and openly wondered whether historic Christianity would survive the attacks of modern theological liberalism. At the heart of this "new orthodoxy," Mullins noted, was a radical form of naturalism that understood everything in terms of "the law of continuity." As a result, "the supernatural is banished" as an explanatory factor and rational naturalism was the controlling presupposition. For the new theologians, Jesus' birth was viewed as natural; his person as divine "only as are other men;" his mission as a religious sage or prophet; his role as an example of "the highest degree of trust in God;" his work as non-miraculous; and his resurrection and ascension as non-historical. However, the "new orthodoxy" was profoundly dishonest in that "it is much given to the use of the old terms, but with new meanings." As a result, "its denials are even more clear and explicit than its affirmations" and New Testament religion was "completely recast."

Mullins extended this critique of theological liberalism in his 1924 book, *Christianity at the Cross Roads*. He held that this radical naturalism that was invading the religious world was the result of science seeking to gain methodological and philosophical dominance. Drawing on nineteenth-century Dutch theologian Abraham Kuyper's thoughts on "sphere sovereignty," Mullins argued that science had crossed out of its sphere and had invaded the spheres of religion and philosophy. By applying the criteria and methodology of science to religion, not only was science remaking religion in its own naturalistic image, but it was also creating "conflict and confusion."

To Mullins, the solution to this conflict between naturalism and supernatural was twofold. First, science, philosophy, and religion had to agree not to overstep their bounds and instead to remain in their respective spheres. After all, each discipline was autonomous, pursuing truth in its own way; each had the right to insist upon "its own rights within its own sphere." Science had "rights" in the area of nature and worked with the principle of causality and development; philosophy's rights were to seek "a single principle to explain the universe;" religion had the right to offer a "personal relation" whose "chief quest is for God and salvation from sin." By remaining in their spheres and pursuing truth in their own way, science, philosophy, and religion could work harmoniously.

Mullins offered a second solution: he insisted on the primacy of the irreducible fact of Jesus Christ in Christian experience and in history. Modern liberalism had no way to meet "the stubborn fact of the sin, guilt, weakness and bondage of man." Modernism simply exhorted men with empty phrases. In contrast, evangelical Christianity proclaimed good news. Those who experienced the reality of God in Jesus Christ were delivered from the power and guilt of sin. This fact of experience was the most powerful apologetic for the truth of Christianity. And so, when people exercised faith in Jesus, experiencing his reality, they knew the true fact of Jesus. This was a fact that could not be explained away by theological liberalism, "scientific absolutism," or rationalistic philosophy.

As Machen read Mullins' defense of the faith offered especially in *Christianity at the Cross Roads*, he deemed it insufficient and even dangerous. In a lengthy review published in 1926 in *Princeton Theological Review*, Machen recognized the significant commonalities between himself and Mullins. Both opposed naturalistic religion and theological liberalism; both upheld the supernaturalism of the Bible; both grounded Christianity in historical realities; hence, both were on the same side in the battle for the Christian faith.

That said, there were significant differences between Machen's and Mullins's defenses of the faith. First, Machen disagreed with Mullins's separation of fact and doctrine, which was ultimately a separation of history from faith. It was not true, according to Machen, "to say that the New Testament presents merely the facts and leaves it to later generations to set forth the meaning of the facts themselves." Rather, the New Testament offers the meaning of those facts—which is doctrine. To divorce fact and doctrine, history from faith, was to occupy the same intellectual ground as the theological liberal.

More troubling was Mullins's "sharp separation between the spheres of science and philosophy and religion." This distinction should logically lead someone into "an abyss of skepticism." By dividing these spheres, Mullins was giving ground to those who argued that the conflict between science and religion might be solved if religion dealt with ideals and spirit and science dealt with facts and phenomena. In contrast, Machen argued that there was no real conflict between science and religion, "not because the Bible does not teach things with which science has a right to deal, but because what the Bible says about these things is true." Far from being a solution or a strong position for defending the faith, the relegation of science, philosophy, and religion into separate spheres actually betrayed Christianity: "For our part we hold that the notion of the distinctiveness of the spheres of science and religion, far from being a great recent gain, is one of the chief forms that have been assumed by modern unbelief, and that its increasing prevalence is one of the most disastrous features of our time."

A final element of disagreement centered on Mullins's separation of doctrine from experience and the resultant exaltation of experience. While Machen agreed with Mullins that Christianity was not merely intellectual, he also believed that the fact that the intellect was insufficient did not render it unnecessary. There was doctrinal content that must be known in order to believe in Jesus Christ. As a result, the basis of evangelism and apologetics should be doctrine defended as the basis for and producer of experience. "We are pleading, in other words, for a truly comprehensive apologetic—an apologetic which does not neglect the theistic proofs or the historical evidence of the New Testament account of Jesus, but which also does not neglect the facts of the inner life of man." For Machen, Mullins's defense of the faith neglected the intellect and started down an "anti-intellectual path" that would ultimately result in the very liberalism that the Southern Baptist decried.

This exchange highlighted Machen's determination to defend the faith on an intellectual basis and to refuse to separate science from religion. And yet, those commitments did not mean that Machen was eager to delve into the debates over evolution, its relationship to Genesis 1, and its propriety as teaching material in public schools. Throughout the 1920s, several states in the American South experienced divisive and bitter public debates over evolution. The most notable was Tennessee, where the infamous "Scopes trial" played out on a national stage. But similar debates were also held in Kentucky, North Carolina, Florida, Mississippi, Arkansas, and Oklahoma; many of these states passed laws that prohibited the teaching of evolution in public schools.

There were several attempts to bring Machen into the fray on one side or the other of the evolution debate; indeed, William Jennings Bryan sought him as an expert witness for the 1925 Scopes Trial. But Machen consistently refused to be drawn too far into these debates. It was not that he found them unimportant or that he had no opinion. As he would put it in 1936, "The Book of Genesis seems to divide the work of creation into six successive steps or stages. It is certainly not necessary to think that the six days spoken of in that first chapter of the Bible are intended to be six days of twenty-four hours each. We may think of them rather as very long periods of time."

However, Machen refused to be drawn into the debates over evolution because he believed that the central issue confronting Christianity was the person and work of Jesus. If Jesus was not who the Bible presented him to be, then it really did not matter how God created the world or how God intended to end it. On the other hand, if Jesus was and did what the Bible said, then the issues surrounding the world's origin and consummation could be rationalized at some level. In order to get at the crucial issues of the person and work of Jesus, one had to be clear about the nature of faith and history. The church's apologetic could not retreat into experience; rather, even its discussion of faith needed to be robustly intellectual and historical. It was this conviction that drove Machen's own apologetic approach in his 1925 book, *What is Faith?*

Picking up the argument that he had offered in *Christianity and Liberalism*—that theological liberalism was both unchristian and unscientific—Machen unpacked the latter claim in *What is Faith?*, namely, that modern theological liberalism was unscientific. By this, he meant that theological liberalism denigrated history and doctrine and instead relied on ineffable religious experiences as both the basis and reason for belief. Such an approach, by definition, was "anti-intellectual" and so "unscientific."

Even worse, such an approach was disastrous for Christianity long-term. For example, the liberal's distinction between religion and theology ultimately produced intellectual skepticism about Christianity itself. Liberals believed that theology was "the changing expression of a unitary experience." As a result, theology "can never be permanent, but is simply the cloth of religious experience in the forms of thought suitable to any particular generation." Such changeable doctrinal belief necessarily led to a devaluing of religious knowledge. In addition, faith so divorced from knowledge "is not faith at all. As a matter of fact, all true faith involves an intellectual element; all faith involves knowledge and issues in knowledge." Faith must have doctrinal content to be true faith.

For this reason, as he had in *Christianity and Liberalism*, Machen set forth various doctrines to demonstrate how necessary they were for modern faith. Against the prevailing pantheism of modern liberalism, he argued that God was a "free Person who can act," who had acted in creating the world, governing all things, and revealing himself to humankind. This God was holy and transcendent, distinct and independent from his creation. "It is because we know certain things about Him, it is because we know that He is mighty and holy and loving," Machen argued, "that our communion with Him obtains its peculiar quality. The devout man cannot be indifferent to doctrine, in the sense in which many modern preachers would have us be indifferent. Our faith in God, despite all that is said, is indissolubly connected with what we *think* of Him."

Against theological liberals who saw Christ as an example of faith, Machen argued that Jesus Christ was the object of faith. As the object of faith, there were many things that people needed to know about Jesus—in particular, his atonement and resurrection. Against those who argued that humankind's great need was to have faith in the divine within, he argued that faith could only be born from a realization of an individual's great need as a sinner. Against liberal theologians who argued that the Cross was an example of self-sacrifice, he claimed that at the Cross, Jesus satisfied the wrath of God and provided salvation for his people. Machen held that saving faith in Jesus' finished work at the Cross brought God's justification to the individual. The justified individual would then produce good works to the glory of God. However, this was the gospel order—faith in Christ produced works for his glory.

As a result, the division theological liberals made between doctrine and experience was anti-intellectual and unscientific. What was needed, Machen argued, was a recovery of the Christian gospel, which had at its heart doctrinal content. A recovery of the gospel would bring a "great revival of the Christian religion; and with it there will come, we believe, a revival of true learning: the new Reformation for which we long and pray may well be accompanied by a new Renaissance." Learning and faith, doctrine and experience, went hand in hand; Machen believed that both were necessary in order to answer the challenge of modernism.

One historical claim in that statement of the Christian gospel was that Jesus was "conceived by the Holy Ghost, born of the Virgin Mary." While some evangelicals simply stated baldly that Jesus was born of the virgin Mary without much historical or biblical rationale and others simply avoided the topic altogether, Machen was determined to demonstrate the rational basis of one of the Bible's most stupendous supernatural claims. As already noted, his interest in the virgin birth went back to his seminary days when he wrote his prize-winning essay as a senior. And his first scholarly articles when he joined the Princeton faculty focused on the birth narratives of Luke.

In his book *The Virgin Birth of Christ*, published in 1930, Machen summarized a lifetime of work on Jesus' birth narratives contained in Matthew and Luke and demonstrated that there were solid historical reasons to accept them at face value. Against those who argued that the virgin birth was a dogmatic belief developed in the second century by Christians looking to support the deity of Jesus, Machen patiently showed that the tradition was neither an addition to the Gospel accounts nor a later development, but organically related to the Gospels themselves. Further, those who attempted to discredit the virgin birth accounts needed to do so on other grounds than those currently used; for the narratives did not bear the marks of Hellenistic Greek thought or middle eastern paganism. The best explanation for the birth narratives was that they presented what actually happened: the Lord visited Mary in a supernatural fashion and caused her to conceive Jesus.

That conclusion particularly made sense, Machen argued, when taken in the light of the Gospel's presentation of Jesus. "The story of the virgin birth, far from being an obstacle to faith, is an aid to faith; it is an organic part of that majestic picture of Jesus which can be accepted most easily when it is taken as a whole," he noted. And especially when one bowed to the authority of the Bible, then the matter was clear, for "everyone admits that the Bible represents Jesus as having been conceived by the Holy Ghost and born of the virgin Mary. The only question is whether in making that representation the Bible is true or false." As he demonstrated throughout his painstaking scholarship, the Bible's presentation of Jesus as virgin-born passes the historical test. Hence, the Bible was true and Jesus was both the person of history and the object of faith.

Such robust intellectual defenses of the faith offered in *What is Faith?* and *The Virgin Birth of Jesus* were a long way from those proposed by E. Y. Mullins and other evangelicals who were willing to accept the epistemology of modernity. For those who were determined to defend the faith, Christian scholarship was an absolutely necessity. While arguments could not transform a person into a Christian, that did not mean that such intellectual defenses were unnecessary. In fact, scholarly, intellectual defenses of the faith were most useful for those who were already believers. That was because they produced "an intellectual atmosphere in which the acceptance of the gospel will be something other than an offense against the truth." And a church where belief is grounded in truth would be prepared to defend the faith against those who undermined it, whether those critics were found within or outside the church.

Indeed, as Machen repeatedly saw during the 1920s, the more dangerous opponents to the Bible were found "within ecclesiastical walls." Machen labored hard to provide strong intellectual arguments for the Christian faith. He was willing to endure controversy in order to defend the truth of God's Word; and he was willing to use "intellectual weapons" to do so. In doing this, Machen fought the good fight of the faith—but what he would find is that fighting the good fight would involve profound risk and costs.

5

Counting the Cost

Even as Machen worked to defend the faith, he was central to the denominational politics within the PCUSA during the 1920s. Seen as a spokesman for "fundamentalists" within his communion and one working to return the church to a more sure theological footing, he would fail to reckon with two realities. The first was the strong denominational loyalty of the vast moderate middle of the Presbyterian church. As conservatives like Machen argued for stricter doctrinal tests for ministers and a more robust confessional identity, the moderates viewed such calls as potentially divisive. As a result, Presbyterian moderates would consistently side with those who affirmed denominational loyalty to be more important than doctrinal purity.

But Machen also failed to reckon with how these debates within the northern Presbyterian church would affect his own beloved Princeton Seminary and eventually his position there. While the seminary held an ascendant and protected position within the church since its founding in 1812, it became more responsive to the church's culture and needs with the presidency of J. Ross Stevenson, which began in 1914. That sense of being the church's seminary, with a responsibility to reflect the diversity of the church in its faculty and perspective, would have significant ramifications as the events of the 1920s unfolded, ones that would ultimately force Machen and his conservative allies to make difficult choices.

By failing to reckon with these twin realities, Machen perhaps misread his own position in the Presbyterian controversy, misused his own prodigious intellectual and rhetorical ability, and relied too much on allies who would be unsteady, all of which would lead to him eventually departing from his beloved Princeton Seminary in 1929. To be sure, the outcome would have probably been the same regardless of what Machen had done: if he had sought to work with, instead of against, his seminary colleague and church opponent Charles Erdman; if he had not involved himself so directly in the political maneuvering; if he had tempered his language and rhetoric. Even if Machen had done all of these things, it is likely that the result would have been the same. Still, the cost was high: Princeton Seminary would be lost to the moderate and liberal factions in the church.

In 1924 it did not look as though this would be the result. Machen's *Christianity and Liberalism* had given a basic framework in defining the issue in the church for Presbyterian conservatives. And when the liberals published the Auburn Affirmation in January 1924, Machen's criticisms seemed prescient: here was clear proof that for theological liberals, doctrines represented the experience of a given generation, not fixed points of biblical understanding. Yet while Machen's case was confirmed, the broad-based support for the Affirmation pointed to how deeply liberalism had taken hold in the church. To Machen, it was clear that conservatives needed to do something or the church would be lost.

Machen's contribution to the conservative cause was a two-part article that was published in April 1924 in *The Presbyterian*. "The Parting of the Ways" suggested that the 1924 General Assembly brought the Presbyterian church to the crossroads: "It may stand for Christ, or it may stand against him; but it can hardly halt between the two opinions." If it stood for Christ, it must do so as a witness to the truth of the New Testament, that "Christ died for our sins according to the Scriptures, that he was buried, and that he rose again the third day according to the Scriptures." Such a stand was not likely in light of what the church had tolerated in its pulpits, especially as evidenced by First Presbyterian Church, New York, and the ministry of Harry Fosdick. Even more, the Presbyterian church had moved toward a false conception of doctrine itself; far too many agreed with Fosdick that "doctrine ... is the expression of Christian experience, and doctrinal controversies may be ended if we will only translate doctrine back into the life from which it came."

In order to move forward as Christ's witnesses, such an understanding of doctrine must be dismantled. Christianity stood robustly for doctrine as objective truths that were true for all time, not just for a particular generation. In fact, Christianity claimed to be in possession of a message that was true. And the church was in the collective enterprise of witness-bearing—the Christian church declared that it possessed a true message about

Jesus to which all people everywhere needed to give obedience. In the Presbyterian church, the way such corporate witness-bearing happened was through the pulpit ministry; those who stood in Presbyterian pulpits claimed to be witnessing to what the church believed about Jesus. Hence, for the pulpit to declare a message that was different from its confessional documents and that was different from historic Christianity was to undermine the church's witness-bearing task.

And so, the question before the church at its upcoming General Assembly was whether it would allow attacks on the Christian faith to continue from its pulpits: and especially whether it would allow the pulpit of First Presbyterian Church, New York, to continue to undermine the faith that the church claimed to hold. Put in the most simple terms, "Would the Church allow Fosdick to continue to preach at First Church, New York, or not? Would the Church continue to allow Fosdick to undermine the historic Christian faith and its corporate witness-bearing?" If the church did not discipline itself and remove Fosdick, then it was taking its stand against Christ and the church would necessarily divide.

By the time Presbyterians gathered in Grand Rapids, Michigan, for the 1924 General Assembly, it appeared that the conservatives were winning the argument in the larger church. Evidence of conservative strength came right at the beginning of the assembly, when Clarence Macartney, pastor of the Arch Street Presbyterian Church in Philadelphia, was elected moderator. This was significant because the moderator had the power to appoint the chairmen of all the assembly committees, which Macartney filled with conservative clergy.

And yet, though conservatives had strength at the assembly, they failed to follow through. Most significantly, the Bills and Overtures Committee recommended no action on an overture from the Presbytery of Cincinnati that recommended some action be taken against the signers of the Auburn Affirmation. In addition, the Assembly failed to deal with the Presbytery of New York, which had ordained men who had denied the virgin birth of Jesus. It further failed to insist that those who worked for denominational agencies reaffirm the 1923 General Assembly's "five points," which had claimed Presbyterian ordination vows demanded belief in the virgin birth of Jesus, the verbal inspiration of the Bible, Jesus' substitutionary atonement and bodily resurrection, and the reality of miracles. And it finally failed to discipline the Presbytery of New York and the First Presbyterian Church there for allowing Fosdick to preach deviant doctrine for several years. The assembly, which should have reformed the church in a more conservative direction, actually was a failure.

That was how Machen viewed the assembly, at least. While he was encouraged by Macartney's election, there were too many failures to view the assembly as a success. "I think that if we represent it as a victory," he wrote to fellow conservative minister Maitland Alexander, "or if we give the impression that we regard the battle as over, we are traitors to our cause." And so, Machen gave a great deal of his efforts over the next year to continuing to promote the conservatives' cause in print and in the pulpit.

One of the more significant statements that Machen made in print during this period was on the topic, "Does Fundamentalism obstruct social progress?" Published in the July 1924 issue of *The Survey Graphic*, Machen cogently argued against common claims against "fundamentalism": namely, that it denied the idea of historical development and progress; that it had a gloomy picture of humankind; and that it overstressed individualism over the social collective. His response to each of these claims tracked similar ground to what he had traversed in *Christianity and Liberalism*: Christianity is a religion based on facts; "all history is based upon a thoroughly static view of facts"; ergo, Christianity is historical and true. Likewise, Christianity was not a religion of "sweet reasonableness based upon confidence in human goodness"; rather, it began with "the consciousness of sin and grounds its hope only in the regenerating power of the Spirit of God." And while "Christianity is social as well as individual," at the end of the day it "insists upon the rights of the individual soul" to repent of sin and believe in Christ for salvation. Such straightforward arguments provided traction with thoughtful people who could see that Machen's fundamentalism was far from obscurantism, but rather was reasonable and articulate.

In early 1925, Machen and several conservative leaders mailed a letter to a thousand Presbyterian conservatives, urging them to continue to work for reform. Mass meetings and plans to elect conservative commissioners to that year's General Assembly were urged. A few months later, Machen preached a sermon in the seminary's Miller Chapel that would later be issued as a pamphlet. Entitled "The Separateness of the Church," Machen preached that "if the sharp distinction is ever broken down between the church and the world, then the power of the church is gone." And yet, such a distinction was happening in the sphere of thought and conduct in the Presbyterian church: "Gradually the church is being permeated by the spirit of the world; it is becoming what the Auburn Affirmationists call an 'inclusive' church." In order to turn the tide and reestablish the separateness of the church, Machen urged his listeners, "Cost what it may, we ought to at least face the facts" about the real condition of the church. And conservatives must pray and work to see reform happen. But there must also be a realistic assessment of what may happen: "It may be that paganism will finally control, and that Christian men and women may have to withdraw from a church that has lost its distinctness from the world." The time for such a withdrawal was nearer than Machen could have known.

As Machen worked to rally conservatives, he was faced with sticky challenges in the context of Princeton Seminary. In fall 1924, the Princeton Students' Association decided to pull out of the Students' Association of Middle-Atlantic Theological Seminaries because the group had "so far departed from the central message of evangelical Christianity" as to make fellowship among theological students "impossible of attainment and practical undesirable." The following spring, the students forged a new relationship with the League of Evangelical Students. What made this difficult was that it offered a public indication of a breach among members of the faculty: in this instance, Charles Erdman, who had been the faculty sponsor of the old organization, and Machen, who nominated Robert Dick Wilson to sponsor the new.

In the midst of this, Erdman became stated supply of the First Presbyterian Church, Princeton. When this happened, Henry van Dyke, the noted liberal Princeton University professor who had left the church publicly during Machen's time as supply, returned to the congregation. This drew the notice of the conservative Presbyterian newspapers. "Does the return of such a pronounced and avowed modernist as Dr. van Dyke to the old church, under the new pastor, mean that he is anticipating more liberal preaching under the new regime?" asked *The Presbyterian*. "Does this action of Dr. van Dyke signify that two parties are developing in the faculty of Princeton Seminary?" Erdman wrote a furious reply published in both religious and secular papers, implying that Machen, as an associate editor of that paper, was somehow responsible for the article and its claims.

Shortly after this exchange, Erdman was once again nominated by the New Brunswick Presbytery to serve as moderator of the General Assembly, hoping for election a year after his defeat by Macartney in 1924. The vote to nominate him was narrow and pointed up again the divisions on the faculty as several Princeton professors, including Machen, voted against nominating Erdman. And Machen took public his opposition to Erdman, writing in *The Presbyterian* that his colleague was the candidate of "the Modernist and indifferentist party in the church." While Erdman was personally orthodox and evangelical, he belonged to that group of evangelical men "who in this great crisis have not the appreciation of the danger in which the church stands to make them safe occupants of the moderator's chair." Machen worried that "a policy of palliation and of compromise will in a few years lead to the control of our church, as has already happened in the case of many churches, by agnostic Modernism." The present was the time for strong men of conviction who would lead the church toward reform.

As historian Bradley Longfield correctly observed, the differences between Machen and Erdman were not personal; they actually had significant differences over what constituted the essence of Christianity and the mission of the church. "For Machen," Longfield observed, "the truth of Christianity was primary doctrinal; for Erdman, existential. For Machen the church's mission was the preservation and probation of true belief; for Erdman its task was to bring men and women into right relation with God. For Machen the church influenced culture by furthering right dogma; for Erdman, the faith ordered society through the lives of redeemed men and women. Though neither would deny the validity of the points the other stressed, differing emphases caused sharp divisions." The problem of the next several years would be that these differing intellectual commitments would be translated as personal; that is, Machen's determined stance would be viewed as an issue of his character, rather than as a matter of principle.

By the time the 1925 General Assembly convened in Columbus, Ohio, the differences between Machen and Erdman, as well as among conservatives, moderates, and liberals in the church, were becoming more plain. Erdman was elected moderator; almost immediately, the church was faced with a complaint regarding the Presbytery of New York's licensure of two men who denied the virgin birth of Jesus, a matter that had come up the previous year. When the Judicial Commission returned an opinion that the presbytery should have deferred licensing these two men because they could not affirm Jesus' virgin birth, it appeared that the liberals might bolt. In response, Erdman proposed a commission of fifteen, that he would appoint "to study the spiritual condition of our Church and the causes making for unrest, and to report to the next General Assembly, to the end that the purity, peace, unity, and progress of the Church may be assured." This proposal passed unanimously, took some of the steam out of the liberals' protest, and blunted any conservative momentum in reforming the church.

When the commission was finally formed, it would have few strong conservatives among its fifteen members. Machen expressed concern about the "partisan character" of the commission; but the truth was that the commission was more loyal than partisan, more denominationally focused than doctrinally concerned. The commission met with Machen in December 1925 and received a short version of his argument from *Christianity and Liberalism*: "Those causes [of unrest] I hold to be all reducible to one great underlying cause—namely, the widespread and in many quarters dominant position in the ministry of the church as well as among its lay membership of a type of thought and experience, commonly called Modernism, which is diametrically opposed to the constitution of our church and to the Christian religion." Such modernism believed that "what is really constant in religion is an inner experience that clothes itself from generation to generation in necessarily changing intellectual forms, so that nothing in the sphere of doctrine can ever be permanently true." Every other disturbance in the life of the church could be traced to this doctrinal cause; any attempt to distract from that issue by blaming those who were calling attention to this problem would simply be unfaithfulness.

In the midst of his argument that theological liberalism

was the real issue disturbing the church, Machen raised another point that perhaps cost him politically with the commission and foreshadowed a future battle that he would undertake. He noted that the denomination's "boards and agencies are signally failing to sound any clear evangelical note in the present time of crisis, when the Christian religion all over the world is in the midst of one of the greatest conflicts in its entire history." By not sounding a clear note that the church stood for a strong proclamation of the gospel of redemption, it was actually in a false position when it came to fundraising and promoting its work. And such doctrinal indifferentism actually forwarded the cause of denominational liberals, who had no problem going forth under the church's auspices to do good to humankind with little interest in declaring a gospel that saves sinners.

To a commission of denominational loyalists—which included the chairman of the Presbyterian Board for Foreign Missions, Robert Speer—Machen's strong condemnation of theological liberalism and indictment of denominational agencies and boards would raise questions. But the questions for denominational loyalists were not about the truth of his characterizations, but about the character of the messenger. When the commission returned its report in 1926, it noted five major causes of unrest in the church: general intellectual movements in the broader culture; historical differences in the church going back to the nineteenth century Old School-New School division; ranging differences over polity, especially concerning the authority of the General Assembly over lower courts and structural issues at the General Assembly itself; theological changes, although none so severe as suggested by Machen and his allies; and misunderstandings fostered by "unfair and untrue statements which have been made in speech and in printed publications." In addition, the commission affirmed that the church had historically embraced doctrinal pluralism within evangelical boundaries: "The Presbyterian system admits of diversity of view where the core of truth is identical," they declared. "Presbyterianism is a great body of belief, but it is more than a belief; it is also a tradition, a controlling sentiment. The ties which bind us to it are not of the mind only; they are ties of the heart as well."

In this commission report, which was approved at the 1926 General Assembly with one dissenting vote, the church issued a strong repudiation of Machen's position. The key cause of unrest in the church was found in those who agitated over doctrinal differences that did not exist and slandered their colleagues in ministry. But those who so agitated failed to recognize that the church had always tolerated a diversity of doctrinal views for the sake of evangelical unity. It was not common belief that bound Presbyterians together, but common sentiment and loyalty to the mission of the church. Hence, according to the commission's report, not only was Machen out of bounds for raising the issues, but more significantly he demonstrated a failure to be truly Presbyterian. And if he did not change his approach, the consequences would be significant.

Indeed, the consequences came at the same General Assembly. Early in 1926, Princeton Seminary's board of directors, who had responsibility for instruction and administration of the theological school, had elected Machen to become professor of Apologetics and Ethics, replacing the retiring William Brenton Greene. According to the school's charter, such appointments had to be approved by the General Assembly, but approval had always been a matter of course. In fact, in the school's history, none of the directors' recommendations had been vetoed. When this matter came before the assembly's Advisory Committee on Theological Seminaries, they heard testimony that reflected negatively on Machen's character: not only was he against the 1919 Volstead Act that prohibited intoxicating beverages and regulated their sale, but his character was also questioned. It was claimed that he was "temperamentally defective, bitter and harsh in his judgment of others and implacable to those who [did] not agree with him." In response to the committee's report, the Assembly took no action on Machen's promotion, which had the net effect of rejecting it.

And yet the consequences did not stop there. The Assembly also granted a request that came from the seminary's president, J. Ross Stevenson, to appoint a special committee to study conditions at the school and to recommend how to work through personal and structural difficulties. This committee would report to the 1927 Assembly and at that time, perhaps, Machen's appointment might be reconsidered. However, the committee seemed much more likely to seek to rectify the faculty division by moving the theological school towards an "inclusivist" position, in which the seminary would "represent the whole Presbyterian church and the spirit of the report of the Commission of Fifteen." The long-term future of Princeton was suddenly at stake: would it continue to be a conservative bastion for the faith or would it succumb to the doctrinal indifferentism that seemed to be winning the day in the Presbyterian church?

6

THE BATTLE OF PRINCETON

From the time Princeton Seminary was founded in 1812, it was a center of theological orthodoxy. As one of the earliest free-standing theological schools in America—only Andover Seminary in 1808 was earlier—it was created in order to produce orthodox ministers, especially because it had become uncertain that Harvard, Yale, or Princeton Colleges could or would ensure their graduates would in fact be orthodox. In addition, Andover and Princeton—and the stream of seminaries after them—typified the growing sense among American Protestants that their ministers needed to have a professional education in the same way that doctors and lawyers did.

As a result, Princeton had a role in producing theologically orthodox, well-equipped, professional ministers for the Presbyterian church and other Protestant communions as well; after all, Baptists and Episcopalians had notable leaders trained at Princeton as well in the antebellum period. And the chief guardians for the orthodoxy of the school were the faculty members.

Starting with the original two faculty members, Archibald Alexander and Samuel Miller, and continuing with Charles Hodge and the subsequent faculty, the faculty had a sense of the importance of their role in preserving and transmitting the Reformed faith to the next generation of ministers. This accounts for Hodge's famous statement, made during the seminary's fiftieth anniversary celebration, that "I am not afraid to say that a new idea never originated in this Seminary."

From the time that Machen began to serve on the faculty of Princeton Seminary in 1906, he cherished that same ideal. While he was trained in the best critical scholarship of the day, he was determined to hold on to and teach Christian orthodoxy, especially as summarized in the Westminster Standards. He had identified himself with the Princeton tradition in such a way that an attack on the seminary was worse than an attack on himself.

That was certainly how he viewed the prospect that the special committee would alter the fundamental character of the seminary. "No doubt I have been at fault in many ways in the matter in which I have tried to maintain what I believe to be right," Machen declared, "but I earnestly hope that my faults may not be allowed to bring harm upon the institution that I love—an institution which is performing today, to a degree attained perhaps never before in its history, a worldwide service in the defense of the Reformed or Calvinistic faith." His fear was not simply for himself, but for the seminary itself.

When the special committee came onto campus in November 1926, they interviewed a wide range of seminary stakeholders: alumni, members of both the boards of trustees and directors, faculty, students. As the conversations unfolded it became clear that there were two sets of issues. The first dealt with governance. From 1824, Princeton had an unusual form of governance involving two boards: the board of trustees, which was responsible for budget and property issues, and the board of directors, which was responsible for instruction and administration. While the arrangement was undoubtedly a bit unwieldy, by the 1920s there were ideological realities in play: for the trustees had a majority of theological progressives, while theological conservatives had the majority of directorship positions. The trustees favored the seminary's president, J. Ross Stevenson, while the directors favored the conservative majority on the faculty and blamed Stevenson for the trouble at the school. As the committee investigated, they became convinced that the two-board structure was part of the difficulty at the school.

The second set of issues involved the faculty. While most of the attention focused on the division between Machen and Erdman, the reality was that the conservative majority was none too pleased with the seminary president either. When the seminary reconvened after the 1926 General Assembly, the faculty took the unprecedented action of censuring Stevenson because of his conduct at the assembly, which demonstrated that he disregarded the proprieties involved in his position as a faculty member. But the committee missed some of the larger difficulties between the president and faculty in their intense focus on Machen and Erdman.

When Machen appeared before the committee, he noted the actions of Stevenson and Erdman at the 1926 Assembly, which resulted in his promotion to the chair of Apologetics and Ethics being held in abeyance. And especially, Machen resented the way his colleagues had attacked his character before the advisory committee on theological seminaries. "I have been subjected to serious obloquy" as a result of their attacks, he observed. While he could defend himself from these charges, he felt it was more important to let the committee understand what he believed the issues dividing the seminary were: "that there is a serious divergence of principle between Dr. Erdman and myself, and that personal unpleasantness was introduced into the discussion of this divergence not by me but by Dr. Erdman."

Machen unpacked the issues of principle, stretching back to the 1920 "Plan of Organic Union" and continuing through Erdman's candidacy for moderator in 1925. At the heart of Machen's perspective was that he was committed to seeking the reformation of the church; Erdman was clear that he was not committed to do this and had in fact defended doctrinal indifferentism; every faculty member should exercise his individual conscience in ecclesiastical matters; hence, Machen opposed Erdman and supported others who worked toward reform. As these matters of principle moved forward, Erdman responded publicly in ways that appeared to be personal attacks upon Machen.

Other faculty members expressed their support and appreciation for Machen. William Park Armstrong, who had recruited Machen to the faculty twenty years before, noted, "Thinking clearly and of strong convictions, [Machen] has not hesitated to state issues with precision; but though his methods of presenting his opinions have seemed to some to be severe, and have been characterized as harsh, they have never descended to the level of personalities." Caspar Wistar Hodge, another New

Testament colleague, observed that "his love and zeal for the truth of the Gospel, his high-mindedness, and his scrupulous fairness toward those holding opposing views have won my admiration." And the directors themselves defended Machen by declaring, "We hold that Dr. Machen has been sorely tried by charges that are false and misleading and we call attention to the fact that those with whom he differs in the church at large, especially in the scholarly world, emphasize his excellent spirit in controversy." This is a far cry from the "temperamentally defective, bitter, harsh, implacable" man about whom Stevenson and Erdman had spoken at the 1926 General Assembly.

It appeared for a moment that the division on the faculty might be bridged. Machen declared that he was open to resume "friendly relations" with Erdman, while the latter admitted that a "bitter, intolerant spirit" had divided them and that he was at fault in this as well. However, by January 1927, the faculty once again divided when Erdman proposed a resolution that suggested the faculty affirm its confidence in each other and in one another's commitment to the seminary's historic doctrinal position. This division—which involved Geerhardus Vos and Caspar Wistar Hodge, along with Machen, opposing Erdman—was ultimately blamed solely on Machen; it was later taken by the special committee as evidence that he was unwilling "to trust the doctrinal loyalties of his colleagues" and that he was "hot footed" in the "intellectual statement of controversy."

When the special committee released its report three weeks prior to the 1927 General Assembly, it blamed the problems at the seminary squarely on Machen and the two-board structure of the school. "The root and source of the serious difficulties at Princeton and the greatest obstacle to the removal of these difficulties, seem to be in the plan of government by two boards," the committee concluded. The committee believed that the division in the faculty mirrored the division between the two boards, with the directors supporting the conservative majority led by Machen and the trustees supporting the moderate minority and the seminary president. By combining the two boards, neither group would have institutional backing; both would have to work through the issues confronted by a single board.

When the 1927 General Assembly received the committee's report, the commissioners debated it at some length. In the end, the committee was continued, expanded to eleven members, and charged with developing recommendations for a new board that would be returned to the following year's assembly. In addition, Machen's promotion, as well as that of O. T. Allis, an Old Testament instructor, continued to be tabled. As could be expected, Machen viewed these developments as "disastrous." If the proposed reorganization occurred, "a new institution of an entirely different type" would replace the Princeton Seminary that Machen had known and loved.

In order to alert the church of the impending danger, Machen wrote and privately published his defense of the seminary. Entitled, "The Attack upon Princeton Seminary: A Plea for Fair Play," the pamphlet was a cry of the heart: the developing sense of loss and grief as the grand old Princeton tradition was going to be undone by a thoughtless reorganization spurred on by a seminary president who had never quite understood the school.

In the pamphlet, Machen notes that "the conservative majority in the board of directors" was the sole reason the school had maintained its historic confessional stance. And while the board of trustees claimed to stand for the "historical theological position of Princeton Theological Seminary," the fact that that board had a signer of the Auburn Affirmation on it demonstrated that the trustees did not quite understand the "Princeton position." To combine these two boards would make the "majority in the affairs of the seminary" the minority, with the result that "the policy of the institution is to be reversed."

In order to make it absolutely clear what the historic position of the theological school was, Machen unpacked the Princeton theology in detail: a stand "for the complete truthfulness of the Bible as the Word of God;" "for the Reformed or Calvinistic faith as being the system of doctrine that the Bible contains;" and the intellectual defense of the Scriptures and the Reformed faith. It was this historic position that the board of directors maintained. Thus, to do away with this board in a single consolidated board was not merely an administrative question; "in reality it is a question upon which the whole character of the institution depends." Maintain the current board of directors and Princeton would continue as a bulwark of the conservative defense of Scripture and the Reformed faith; do away with that board, "and the fine old institution, with all its noble traditions, will be dead."

The demise of Princeton Seminary would not only be disastrous for the Presbyterian church. It would affect "the future of evangelical Christianity." To this point, Princeton had been the thought-leader for evangelicals around the world. Even those who opposed Princeton's position on the inerrant Word recognized its defense of the Scriptures—through the Hodges, Warfield, and W. H. Green—as credible. Its propagation of Reformed Christianity had impacted churches from Scotland and Ireland to South Africa to New Zealand and Australia. And men from every Protestant denomination had received training from Princeton Seminary. Indeed, "never has the prestige of our ancient institution been quite so wide as it is today," he noted. "It is almost pathetic to observe the eagerness with which Princeton is looked to by men all over the world who in the face of the prevailing Modernist tyranny love the Bible as the Word of God and cherish the full gospel of the Lord Jesus Christ."

If the modernists and the indifferentists in the Presbyterian church conspired to destroy Princeton Seminary, Machen warned, Presbyterian evangelicals would have to consider what ought to be done. "One thing, of course, is clear—there will be imperative need of a truly evangelical seminary to take the place of the institution that will have been lost," he declared. That future institution "shall contend earnestly for the faith" and not conceal the issue in the Presbyterian church and in evangelical Protestantism at large. But the time for a new institution was not yet, he held; Princeton Seminary might still be saved "if the evangelical people in our church had any understanding of what is going on." All would hinge on the 1928 Assembly defeating the recommendations that were sure to come from the expanded committee.

In the event, Machen's pamphlet did not change hearts or opinions. By the time the committee reported to the 1928 General Assembly meeting in Tulsa, Oklahoma, all of the sides of the issue had been aired. And as it happened, the assembly had majority and minority recommendations to consider. All but one of the committee members signed off on recommendations to form a single board of trustees and allow this committee to make nominations for this new board. The single dissenting committee member, Ethelbert D. Warfield, objected to the majority's plan, criticizing both the expansion of the seminary president's powers and the method of choosing board members. The assembly approved the majority plan for a single board and instructed the committee to make recommendations for constituting the new board to be considered by the court the following year.

However, waiting until 1929 simply delayed the inevitable. When the matter of the seminary's reorganization came to the assembly floor, only twenty-five minutes were allotted to the matter. Machen was only allowed five minutes to address the gathering in St. Paul, Minnesota. His words were less argument, more eulogy and plea. Speaking of the injustice of the reorganization, he noted, "There are many of Christ's little ones whom the injustice of it grieves to the very heart ... It is hard for me to look into your faces and see many of you ready to do that ruthless thing which, if you only knew its meaning, you would be the first to abhor." And yet, this ruthless thing was simply "a typical example of the same old story, so often repeated, of an institution formerly evangelical that is being made to drift away by insensible degrees from the gospel that it was founded by godly donors to maintain." After Machen's speech, the assembly voted for the special committee's report and established the new board with two signers of the Auburn Affirmation as trustees.

With the creation of a single board for the seminary,

Machen was thrown in a quandary. Should he remain at Princeton and soldier on for evangelical truth? Or should he do what he had hinted and form a new evangelical Presbyterian seminary that would serve as the continuation of the Princeton tradition? It seems that he had determined the answer to the first question relatively quickly: he would not serve under the new board. And the idea of a new seminary began to take shape in the summer months of 1929: perhaps "a really evangelical Seminary might be the beginning of a really evangelical Presbyterian church." The key would be finding faculty members at short notice and forming a board that would support a new endeavor that would be based inside the bounds of the conservative Philadelphia Presbytery.

As the new board came into place, four current Princeton faculty members refused to continue to serve further: Machen, O. T. Allis, Robert Dick Wilson, and Cornelius Van Til. These four men, along with Ned Stonehouse, Allan MacRae, Paul Woolley, and R. B. Kuiper, became the original faculty of the newly formed Westminster Theological Seminary. This faculty was joined by fifty students, including several who would have been seniors at Princeton Seminary, most notably Harold John Ockenga and Carl McIntire. Meeting in the Witherspoon Building in downtown Philadelphia, the new theological school held its opening exercises on September 25, 1929.

At that first convocation, Machen laid out his own understanding of Westminster Seminary's place within theological education, the Presbyterian church, and evangelical Protestantism. At the center and core of this new theological school was the Bible; the school's goal was to produce "specialists in the Bible." In order to do this, the curriculum was unabashedly designed to focus on the Bible and its interpretation: study of the original languages of Greek and Hebrew, biblical exegesis and interpretation, and biblical theology. Likewise, other auxiliary studies such as apologetics, church history, and homiletics were vital parts of the school's design. But the "center of the seminary's course" was systematic theology. For in this study was the conviction that "God has given us not merely theology, but a system of theology, a great logically consistent body of truth." This system, which was summarized in the Westminster Standards, was the focus of all biblical study and the system that Westminster Seminary meant to inculcate. While men from other denominations and traditions were welcome at this new seminary, they needed to know that the school would be committed to setting forth "that great historic faith that has come through Augustine and Calvin to our own Presbyterian church."

As it would turn out, many students would come to Westminster Seminary in order to learn the Reformed faith as it was held in the Princeton tradition. The wonder of it all is that the theological school remains in approximately the same place theologically and ecclesiastically in which Machen and the founding faculty started it nearly eighty years ago. To be sure, this has not been without struggle and difficulty. Still, one would think that Machen would be pleased to see his theological school continuing to stand for the Bible and the Reformed faith, teaching it to evangelical Presbyterians and others who would learn the gospel there. While the battle for Princeton was lost, in God's mercy, the cause of Princeton continues in the classrooms of the school that Machen built.

7

Rethinking Missions

It was not obvious in 1929 that Machen would see the need to form a new Presbyterian mission board. After all, he had invested a great deal of financial and relational capital in starting Westminster Seminary; his experience and interests were connected to theological education, not international missions; and his conservative supporters, such as Clarence Macartney, had swallowed hard to support his new theological school.

Four years later, Machen had started the Independent Board for Presbyterian Foreign Missions. And while the steps to the creation of this new mission board may not have been obvious, there was a marriage between Machen's distrust of the Presbyterian Board for Foreign Missions and especially the board's secretary, Robert E. Speer, and Machen's concern about the orthodoxy of Presbyterian missionaries, especially the famous author Pearl Buck. As distrust and concern came together, Machen decided to act.

Machen's distrust of the Presbyterian Board for Foreign Missions went back at least to 1925. At that point, he had confessed, "It is not now contrary to my conscience to give to our Foreign Board, though I cannot say that I give with much enthusiasm." While he continued to support the board, Machen had to have been soured by Speer's involvement on the Special Commission of 1925 and especially his authorship of the commission's report, which had largely whitewashed the issue of liberalism in the church and had turned the church's bureaucratic force toward Princeton Seminary. In addition, Speer was moderator of the 1927 General Assembly, which approved the commission's final report, and served on the Princeton Seminary board of trustees, throwing his support to the seminary president and the forces of change.

By early 1929, Machen exchanged letters with a board employee, Lindsay Hadley, who oversaw missions candidates. Though the exchange started with questions about the eligibility of Princeton students who had served internships with the Presbyterian Church of Canada, over time the letters focused on Machen's general dissatisfaction with the board as a whole. Later that spring, he summarized many of these concerns in an essay—"Can Evangelical Christians Support our Foreign Board?"—and mailed it to Speer.

Machen's concerns centered on three main areas. The first was the candidacy process, which he believed to be prejudiced against those who held a robustly confessional version of the Reformed faith. A second set of concerns focused on the make-up of the board itself, which included four who had signed the Auburn Affirmation; and this count did not include Hadley, the candidate secretary, who had also signed that document. A mixed board—including moderates and doctrinal indifferentists—could not adequately promote a gospel-focused missions agenda. Finally, Machen raised questions about Speer's 1929 book, *Are Foreign Missions Done For?* When the book discussed Christian doctrine, Machen believed that Speer was "dishearteningly evasive and vague." By using "ambiguous language," the foreign missions board had created a platform that could include conservatives, moderates and liberals on the same mission field.

Machen continued his focus on Speer's theological perspective and, by extension, his leadership of the foreign mission board. The following year, he wrote a lengthy review of Speer's book, *Some Living Issues*. At the heart of Machen's objection to Speer's book was this: "Dr. Robert E. Speer shows himself in this book to be, as indeed he has with increasing clearness become, a representative of that tendency in the church which seeks to mediate and obscure an issue about which we think that a man must definitely take sides." And the issue of the day was between "Christianity as set forth in the Bible and the great creeds of the church and a non-doctrinal or indifferentist Modernism that is represented in the Presbyterian Church in the U.S.A. by the 'Auburn Affirmation.'" In Machen's view, Speer stood on the side of the doctrinal indifferentists who constitute "the most serious menace to the life of the church today."

For evidence of Speer's doctrinal indifferentism, Machen unpacked the problems with *Some Living Issues*, often in excruciating detail. The net effect of the demonstration was to show that while Speer himself might be personally orthodox, his understanding of how to present the gospel to the lost world—and even what that gospel was—was lacking. Indeed, the book consisted of two contradictory strains, evangelical Christianity married to the language and forms of theological liberalism. And if this was a representation of the secretary's thinking, then what effect did this have on the work of the mission board? What kind of missionaries was serving the church when such doctrinal vagueness and inconsistency was represented at the top of the organization?

There was soon an answer to the question of the kind of missionaries who were serving the Presbyterian church. The occasion was the publication of the 1932 book, *Re-Thinking Missions*. The book had its origin in a study commissioned and bankrolled by J. D. Rockefeller, Jr., in partnership with other Baptist laymen, that investigated Protestant missions after one hundred years of investment in the cause. This "laymen's report" was collated with a separate project led by a board of appraisal headed by Harvard professor William Ernest Hocking. The final report spanned seven volumes and the key findings were summarized in this single book.

The theological sections of the book, authored by Hocking, argued that Christianity's significance was not to be found as an exclusivist pathway to salvation through faith in Jesus Christ. Rather, it was to be seen "in its selection of truths available in all religions and in the simplicity of its central teachings." In other words, Christianity's value was as the supreme integration point for all world religions. Missions, then, should be focused on "promoting world understanding on the spiritual level" through service of others, not through proselytization of the "lost."

Most mainline Protestant missions agencies, including the Presbyterian Board for Foreign Missions, had supported the Rockefeller-Hocking project at the beginning, but quickly distanced themselves from the project after the publication of *Re-Thinking Missions.* That probably would have sufficed if Presbyterian missionary and novelist Pearl Buck had remained silent.

However, Buck reviewed the book for the liberal Protestant magazine, *Christian Century,* and gave it a ringing endorsement. "I have not read merely a report," she gushed. "I have read a unique book, a great book. The book presents a masterly statement of religion in its place in life, and of Christianity in its place in religion." In fact, she further noted, "I think this is the only book I have ever read which seems to me literally true in its every observation and right in its every conclusion." Not only did Buck agree with the theological argument, but also the practical application: "Above all, let the spread of the spirit of Christ be rather by mode of life than preaching. I am weary to death with this incessant preaching ... Let us cease our talk for a time and cut off our talkers, and try to express our religion in terms of living service, so that we may show others and see for ourselves if our religion is worth anything or not." One could hardly imagine a stronger endorsement of *Re-Thinking Missions.*

Buck was not finished. Two months after her review, she published another article, this time in *Harper's* magazine, on "Is there a case for foreign missions?" Originally delivered as a speech to Presbyterian women and members of the foreign missions board, Buck answered that there was a case for international missions, but on a different basis than conservative evangelicals supposed. If missions were simply conceived as preaching the gospel and telling internationals that they are going to hell if they do not believe in Jesus, then, no, Buck argued, there was no case for such missionary work. If, on the other hand, missions were viewed as inculcating the spirit of Jesus in serving others and reforming civilizations based on that spirit, then and only then was missionary work worthwhile.

Machen led the reaction against *Re-Thinking Missions* and Pearl Buck's defense of it. The Rockefeller-Hocking project, Machen noted, "constitutes from beginning to end an attack upon the historic Christian faith. It presents as the aim of missions that of *seeking* truth together with adherents of other religions rather than that of *presenting* the truth which God has supernaturally recorded in the Bible." Equally troubling was the tepid response from the Presbyterian Board for Foreign Mission: the board "failed to utter any ringing disapproval of its central position and contented itself with a vague statement concerning its loyalty to the evangelical basis of the missionary enterprise." Such a failure was not surprising, he observed, because the candidate secretary was a signer of the Auburn Affirmation and presumably held attitudes toward doctrine that were similar to those found in *Re-Thinking Missions*.

In reference to Pearl Buck, Machen was complimentary in a backhanded way: "One thing is certainly to be said for Mrs. Buck. She is admirably clear. Her utterances are as plain as the utterances of our Board of Foreign Missions are muddled. There is nothing vague or undecided about them. She has let it be known exactly where she stands. She is opposed to the old gospel and is not afraid to say so in the presence of all the world." The problem was that Buck remained a Presbyterian missionary even with her forthright rejection of cardinal Christian doctrines. What would the board do about Pearl Buck: would they ignore her and so condone with their silence her beliefs? Or would they dismiss her?

In order to press the issues, Machen introduced an overture to the New Brunswick Presbytery, supported by a lengthy document that was mailed to all the members of the court as well as the foreign missions board. The overture would have requested the General Assembly "to take care to elect to positions on the Board of Foreign Missions only persons who are fully aware of the danger in which the Church stands" and who are determined to insist on the cardinal doctrinal commitments such as the "full truthfulness of Scripture," the virgin birth of Jesus, his substitutionary atonement and bodily resurrection as well as his miracles. These board members would insist on these beliefs not only for themselves, but also for all Presbyterian missionaries and board staff, especially the candidate secretary.

Machen's overture was docketed for the April 1933 meeting of the New Brunswick Presbytery and board secretary Robert Speer was invited to be present and to respond. When the presbytery gathered at Trenton for its April meeting, many were expecting a theological debate. When Machen spoke on behalf of his overture, the effect was electric: "Here was true eloquence," said one observer; "Not the eloquence of the facile phrase and the sonorous period, but the eloquence of deep smoldering moral earnestness that now blazed up like a consuming fire and now flashed downward like a shining sword." In response, though, Speer read from a prepared statement that failed to respond to anything Machen said or to anything found in his mailed booklet. Instead, the missions secretary argued against the constitutionality of Machen's overture and broadly defended the soundness of the board and the evangelical zeal of the church. Speer's defenders carried the day: the presbytery voted down Machen's overture and passed a resolution affirming confidence in the foreign missions board.

Though the overture failed in New Brunswick Presbytery, some of Machen's allies in Philadelphia Presbytery were able to secure its passage: it would come before the 1933 General Assembly. In fact, seven separate overtures came to the General Assembly that referenced *Re-Thinking Missions* and the work of the board in some fashion. Prior to the assembly, Pearl Buck resigned her position as a Presbyterian missionary, a resignation that the Presbyterian Board of Foreign Missions received "with deep regret." However, Buck's absence did not abate the larger concerns that conservatives had about the board.

In the end, however, the 1933 Assembly was a massive defeat for Machen and for the conservative cause. The Standing Committee of Foreign Missions, which reviewed the work of the foreign missions board, had received an extensive packet of information from Speer regarding the seven overtures that they had received from the presbyteries. In response, the committee produced majority and minority reports. The majority report, which represented forty-three of the forty-five members of the committee, "reaffirmed the church's adherence to its standards, expressed its confidence in the orthodoxy of Speer and the Board of Missions, and repudiated all theological statements in *Re-Thinking Missions* that conflicted with the theological positions of the church." The minority report argued that the charges made by Machen in his supporting documents were true, urged the assembly to deplore the acts and policies of the board that had caused the controversy, and sought to commit the church to change the members of the board by electing new conservative members for the class of 1936. The assembly rejected the minority report and affirmed the majority report overwhelmingly; and when Robert Speer came to give his report on his activities as senior secretary of the board, he was met with a standing ovation.

Machen's response to his defeat was swift. At the assembly itself, a new missions agency was in the works, the Independent Board for Presbyterian Foreign Missions. This new board, which had fifteen ministers, five elders, and five women in its original form, elected Machen as its president in October. And though this new board sought to be truly Presbyterian even though independent from the denominational organization, it came to be extremely divisive for Presbyterian conservatives. As historian D. G. Hart observed, "Forming the new board was also an act of desperation. For even though Machen believed he had not violated church law, the renegade missions agency strained his own understanding of Presbyterian procedure. The board was clearly designed to expose the tyranny of the denomination's bureaucracy and divide the church between liberals and conservatives. As a result, he lost most of his credibility within the denomination."

Indeed, erstwhile supporters began to turn on Machen as a result of his championing this new missions board. In his own presbytery, Caspar Wistar Hodge, who had supported Machen while they were on the faculty at Princeton, urged the court to amend its rules to require ministers transferring into the presbytery or ordinands and licentiates seeking credentials to affirm support and loyalty to the denomination's boards and agencies. Clarence Macartney, now pastor of First Presbyterian Church, Pittsburgh, Pennsylvania, also refused to join and in time would leave the Westminster Seminary board because of these activities.

The tension that this board represented was that it was "independent" and yet "Presbyterian." To most conservative Presbyterians, those two words together seemed to be an oxymoron. As Macartney would later reflect, "If [Machen] had named it the Independent Board for Foreign Missions, or the Evangelical Board for Foreign Missions, or some similar name, the result might have been different. But when he called it the Independent Board for Presbyterian Foreign Missions he gave his enemies an opening of which they at once availed themselves." The new board's independency attracted a range of maverick types who rallied to Machen because he stood against the denominational drift, not because they were committed to his vision. The new board's Presbyterianism left it open to being declared schismatic for its willingness to divert money away from the denomination's boards and agencies to its own cause.

As it so happened, that is exactly what happened. Just a month after Machen was elected president of the new missions agency, the moderator of the General Assembly and one of the secretaries of the foreign missions board, John McDowell, suggested publicly that the Independent Board was unconstitutional. By the time the 1934 General Assembly convened in Cleveland, the Assembly's General Council had circulated its study of the issues that claimed "the broadest possible construction [of] the General Assembly's powers and centralized the workings of the denomination." In fact, the study claimed that failing to give to and support the denomination's agencies and boards was equivalent to a church member refusing to participate in the Lord's Supper. Such was the strong case made for denominational loyalty: it made giving to the church's agencies a kind of means of grace.

And so, when the Assembly issued its "mandate" in response to the new board, it should not have been surprising. The mandate required that the Independent Board for Presbyterian Foreign Missions dissolve, that all Presbyterian ministers and church members disassociate from it, and that any who refused to separate themselves from this board would be subject to the discipline of the church. Further, presbyteries were urged to proceed to bring charges of disorderly conduct and disloyalty to ordination vows against those who refused to leave the board.

From the perspective of Presbyterian history, it should be obvious that the Assembly's "mandate of 1934" was just as heavy-handed and unconstitutional as the Old School Presbyterian actions in the Old School-New School division in 1837. However, what was equally obvious was that the Assembly had affirmed two positions: loyalty to the denomination's agencies and programs made one a Presbyterian and doctrinal pluralism was acceptable as long as one affirmed the significance of Jesus Christ in some fashion. In twelve short years—from 1922, when Harry Emerson Fosdick had asked the question, "Shall the Fundamentalists Win?"—the church had defined itself in ways that made it impossible for those who held doctrinal particularity to be more significant than denominational loyalty to remain. It was a small step from there to a truly Presbyterian church.

8

A TRUE PRESBYTERIAN
CHURCH

Machen believed that the 1934 Assembly's mandate was blatantly unconstitutional. He was determined not to obey the demand. But his personal situation made things a bit confusing. A few months before the Assembly met, Machen had secured a transfer of his ministerial membership from the New Brunswick Presbytery to the Philadelphia Presbytery. All of this was handled according to the rules of the Book of Church Order and seemed in order.

However, the minority who had voted against receiving Machen into Philadelphia Presbytery filed a complaint, which was formally presented to the presbytery and then sent on to the Synod of Pennsylvania. The minority argued that such a complaint prevented Machen from being part of the Philadelphia Presbytery until the synod ruled on the matter; Machen and the majority argued that he was part of the presbytery unless the synod overruled the action.

The confusion of Machen's presbytery membership would become significant as the wheels of discipline began to move. New Brunswick Presbytery acted as though it had original jurisdiction; as a result, in September 1934, it appointed a committee to investigate the matter and to determine how to act on Machen's case. When Machen finally met the committee in December, he had a prepared statement, which he later printed and distributed at his own cost.

His response to the Assembly's mandate was forthright: "I cannot obey the order," he wrote simply. The mandate not only would have forced Machen and other conservatives to support "propaganda that is contrary to the gospel of Christ," but more significantly it would have involved "substitution of a human authority for the authority of the Word of God." To disobey the Assembly's mandate was allowable because the mandate was unconstitutional, Machen noted; he was still "in accord with the constitution of that church and can appeal from the General Assembly to the Constitution."

In the rest of his statement, Machen unpacked these claims in great detail. Ultimately, however, his pleadings fell upon deaf hears. Eight days later, when New Brunswick Presbytery met in Trenton, they formally appointed a judicial commission that laid the following charges against him: "With the violation of his ordination vows; with his disapproval of the government and discipline of the Presbyterian Church; with renouncing and disobeying the rules and lawful authority of the Church; with advocating rebellious defiance against the lawful authority of the Church; with refusal to sever his connection with the 'Independent Board for Presbyterian Foreign Missions' as directed by the General Assembly; with not being zealous and faithful in maintaining the peace of the church; with contempt of and rebellion against his superiors in the church in their lawful counsels, commands, and corrections; with breach of his lawful promises; with refusing subjection to his brethren in the Lord." All of these charges stemmed from Machen's one act of refusing to obey the Assembly's mandate that the Independent Board dissolve and that he separate from it.

Once the charges were filed and the trial began in February 1935, the question of Machen's presbytery membership once again became germane. Even though New Brunswick Presbytery had dismissed Machen and Philadelphia Presbytery had received him, leading to a complaint against that action before the Synod of Pennsylvania, the prosecution argued and the judicial commission agreed that New Brunswick Presbytery had jurisdiction over Machen and had the right to try him. Once the commission determined that it had the right to try Machen, it became clear that the trial's end was already predetermined.

If there was any doubt, it was removed when, upon hearing Machen's plea of not guilty of the seven charges, the commission ruled not to admit any arguments connected to the Auburn Affirmation, the theological commitments of the Presbyterian Board of Foreign Missions, or the legality and constitutionality of the Assembly's 1934 mandate. He was simply not allowed to present any evidence that was germane to his own defense. As one biographer noted, "Thus with one stroke Machen was denied the right of having his day in court to prove that the order which he disobeyed was an unlawful order."

In this light, the rest of the trial became a farce. The prosecution presented evidence that showed that Machen was connected with the board and refused to separate from it; hence, he was guilty of disobeying the Assembly's 1934 mandate. Since Machen was unable to present any explanation or information or challenge, the defense simply rested. And when the judicial commission gave their guilty verdict at the end of March 1935 and suspended Machen from ministry, even liberal Presbyterians recognized how unfair the trial had been. For example, Daniel Russell, pastor of the Rutgers Presbyterian Church, told the *New York Times* that "there are doctrinal differences which run to the heart of the entire problem. These the accused was not permitted to discuss in his defense."

The great irony was that the New Brunswick Presbytery disciplined Machen because he refused to dissolve the Independent Board and so was disobedient to the General Assembly, but the New York Presbytery had protected Henry P. Van Dusen when they had licensed him even though he denied the virgin birth of Jesus and was disobedient to the Assembly's deliverance of 1923. One cannot help but believe that the show trial that Machen received was less about the issue at hand and more the climax of thirteen years of dissension and agitation. The typically slow-moving Presbyterian disciplinary process moved fairly quickly to excise Machen from the church.

Of course, there was yet one more step in the process. Machen had the right of appeal to the General Assembly's Permanent Judicial Commission. He did appeal to the assembly's commission, which did not receive the case until after the 1935 General Assembly, meaning that it would hear it the following year. The 1935 Assembly featured no less than thirteen separate overtures or resolutions related to the Independent Board specifically or to the church's missions program generally. Nearly half of these overtures urged the church to ensure that its mission program be in conformity with biblical and confessional mandates. The other half of the overtures urged the church to stop prosecuting those associated with the new missions board and to rescind the mandate of 1934. Yet while these overtures signaled the mind of a portion of the church, those set against the Independent Board were even more determined to root out its influence and presence from the church. Three commissioners who were members of the Independent Board were refused enrollment in the assembly even though they were ministers in good standing against whom no disciplinary action had been brought. As one observer noted, "When the assembly ousted these three ministers by a majority vote it exhibited the worst kind of tyranny."

Such actions demonstrated that the Assembly's judicial commission was unlikely to be any more friendly to Machen's case than his presbytery was. In many ways, Machen was counting on this; he had already set in motion the necessary machinery to form a new denomination. After the 1935 Assembly met, Machen and others organized the Constitutional Covenant Union. This association ostensibly existed to protest the aggressive and unconstitutional actions of the PCUSA General Assembly; but from its preamble, it was clear that it served as the initial structure for a new denomination. The Covenant Union defended the Bible, the Westminster Standards, and Presbyterian polity and pledged itself to seek to reform the mainline church but also to prepare "to perpetuate the true Presbyterian Church in the U.S.A. regardless the cost."

Other conservatives were not convinced that creating a shadow structure that would become a new denomination was the best strategy. Samuel Craig, the editor of *Christianity Today*, believed that the Covenant Union erred in committing its members to withdraw should the appeals of Machen and others be denied. Likewise, Clarence Macartney offered to defend Machen before the assembly's judicial commission, an offer that Machen declined "saying that if I defended him, he might be acquitted, and that was not what he wanted. He had already made up his mind to secede." But such a secession, in Macartney's mind, would prove to be "abortive" and fail to achieve Machen's plans and expectations. Most painfully, there was a division among the Westminster Seminary faculty and board over the Independent Board and the new Covenant Union, which resulted in the resignation of Old Testament faculty member, O. T. Allis, and thirteen trustees, including Macartney.

This division in opinion over the wisdom of the Covenant Union and its commitment to withdraw "to perpetuate" the true Presbyterian church signaled again the deep division among conservatives and pointed to the general lack of support that Machen had for his new structures. While Westminster Seminary was limping along producing eight graduates a year, the Independent Board for Presbyterian Foreign Missions supported eleven missionaries. And the Covenant Union initially only had 100 members in its original formation. It seems clear that there was not much enthusiasm for leaving the mainline Presbyterian church regardless of how much conservatives disliked its leftward movement.

And yet, Machen and his allies pressed on. They formed a new magazine that would serve as the mouthpiece of the new Covenant Union, the *Presbyterian Guardian*. The early issues served as a series of indictments of the mainline Presbyterian Church's agencies and boards: exposes of modernism and the Board of Christian Education, modernism and the Board of National Missions, and modernism and the Board of Foreign Missions. While the ostensible purpose of this exposure was to bring about reform in the PCUSA, it also had the added benefit of making the case for a new denomination should the expected happen and Machen and the other Independent Board members be suspended and deposed from ministry.

The 1936 General Assembly, which began on May 28 in Syracuse, New York, was anticlimactic. The Permanent Judicial Commission heard the cases of Machen and seven others ministers associated with the Independent Board; its verdict was for the New Brunswick Presbytery to suspend Machen immediately from ministry. But before that could happen, the Constitutional Covenant Union held a convention on June 11–14, 1936, in Philadelphia, and formed itself into a new denomination, the Presbyterian Church of America (the church would change its name to the Orthodox Presbyterian Church in 1939).

Machen was elected moderator of this first constituting assembly of the new Presbyterian denomination. When he stood to deliver his moderator's sermon, he looked out over a church that consisted of thirty-four ministers and seventeen elders, which represented around 5,000 communicant members. And yet, far from being discouraged, Machen was exultant: "We became members, at last, of a true Presbyterian Church; we recovered, at last, the blessing of true Christian fellowship. What a joyous moment it was! How the long years of struggle seemed to sink into nothingness compared with the peace and joy that filled our hearts!"

Machen's sermon reinforced this sense that the tiny breakaway group was in fact a "real branch of the Church universal, a real part of the Church of God." It was the case that this new denomination would not have much in the way of property, influence, or power; in that regard, it shared the same existence as the early church. In Ephesus, Machen observed, one would not have seen large edifices; rather, the church was different: "Little groups of humble people, without great buildings, meeting here in an upper room, there perhaps at spare hours in a rhetorician's school. Yet it was the Church of the living God, the temple of the Holy Ghost."

Undoubtedly, Machen stressed these biblical realities because he knew that creating a new denomination, especially one made up initially of seceding congregations from the mainline body, would be costly: small churches, no property, lost friendships and associations. And yet, this was the cost of faithfulness to Christ. To be sure, it was a cost that many conservatives in the PCUSA were unwilling to pay—instead, they were content to remain in the church, doing "evil that good may come," submitting to liberal propaganda and supporting agencies that were subverting the gospel. For Machen and the newly formed Presbyterian Church of America, the choice was clear: they would listen to Christ's voice, not the deceptive voice of Satan that urged compromise with liberalism.

Although the new denomination was standing for Christ and was part of the church universal, it already experienced a division at its first assembly. The issue was which version of the Westminster Standards would the new church adopt: would it adopt the original American version of the Standards from 1789 or would it adopt the amended 1903 version that included two additional chapters on the Holy Spirit and missions? Some argued that the Presbyterian Church of America stood as the true spiritual and legal successor of the "apostate" PCUSA; hence, it needed to adopt the same standards in order to make that case, especially before the law courts as congregations fought for their property. Others claimed that the 1903 amendments and additions served as a marker of the doctrinal downgrade in the mainline church; in order to signal the new denomination's confessional, orthodox position, it needed to return to the original American version of the doctrinal standards. The issue was not settled in June, but awaited the second General Assembly, which would be held in November.

The rest of 1936 made it plain that not everyone who was present at the founding assembly had the same vision for what a "true Presbyterian Church" would be. All who joined this small band of congregations stood against the theological liberalism of the PCUSA. But some were determined that the new church would be a conservative mainline church: loyal to the Westminster Standards while allowing diversity on less important doctrinal issues such as eschatology; expansive in its plans for evangelism and cultural engagement; ecumenical in its cooperation with the fundamentalist-evangelical coalition. Others rejected this vision for their church for a more limited, confessional one: closer adherence to the Westminster Standards; thoroughly Reformed in its church life, missions, and evangelism; more discriminating in its approach to ecumenism and cultural engagement.

Historian George Marsden noted that the conflict between these two visions eventually came to be expressed in three major issues: eschatology, Presbyterian polity, and Christian liberty. The first issue, eschatology, came up in September 1936. R. B. Kuiper, professor of practical theology at Westminster Seminary, wrote a report for the Christian Reformed Church's newspaper on the first assembly of the new Presbyterian church. In that report, he observed that "it would have warmed the cockles of any Christian Reformed minister to hear how closely [new ordinands] were questioned about the two errors which are so extremely prevalent among American fundamentalists, Arminianism and the Dispensationalism of the Scofield Bible." Almost immediately, Carl McIntire objected in the pages of his *Christian Beacon* newspaper, suggesting that Kuiper's comments were a veiled attack on all those in the new denomination who held to premillennialism.

Machen moved quickly to try to put out the fire, writing an editorial in the *Presbyterian Guardian* and assuring premillennialists that they had a place in the new church. While on the surface, a strict reading of the Westminster Larger Catechism would seem to rule out premillennialism, Machen noted that "subscription to the Westminster Standards in The Presbyterian Church of America is not to every word in those Standards, but only to the *system* of doctrine which the Standards contain." In the light of this, the real question was whether a premillennialist could hold the system of doctrine contained in the Standards. Machen's answer was: "We think that he can; and for that reason we think that Premillennialists as well as those who hold the opposing view may become ministers or elders or deacons in The Presbyterian Church of America."

But Machen was also careful to distinguish between premillennialism and dispensationalism. Premillennialism simply held that Jesus would return before a thousand-year period known as the millennium and that the resurrection would be in two stages, the righteous raised before the millennium when Jesus returned and the rest of humankind raised after the thousand-year period to face the judgment. Dispensationalism, as represented especially in the popular Scofield Reference Bible, posited that there was a stark division between Old Testament Israel and the New Testament church, that there were two ways of salvation, with Israel being saved by law and the church saved by grace, and that there would be a "secret rapture" of believers before a seven-year period called the Tribulation. Machen viewed all of these teachings found in the Scofield Bible to be "profoundly harmful." The new church would certainly have room for premillennialists, but not for dispensationalists.

Presbyterian polity would be the next issue to bedevil the new church. There were two issues along this line. The first dealt with the adoption of the Westminster Standards. The committee entrusted with this recommendation urged the second General Assembly to adopt the 1789 version of the Standards and reject the 1903 amendments. This was certainly Machen's own position, expressed before the Second Assembly: "The more we review the history of the Presbyterian Church in the U.S.A., the more we are inclined to think that perhaps the really decisive step in the downward path was the adoption of the amendments to the doctrinal Standards of the Church in 1903." Hence, the path toward reformation was to reject those amendments and to return to a robust confessionalism. The church followed Machen and its committee's lead and adopted the older version of the doctrinal standards.

However, those frustrated by the increasingly explicit Presbyterian character of the new church worked to seize control of the Independent Board for Presbyterian Foreign Missions, leading to a second polity problem. Machen's intention for the Independent Board was that it stand as a temporary measure; it was likely that he would have recommended that the Independent Board be merged into whatever missions committee or agency the new Presbyterian Church of America would create. However, that opportunity never came. During the annual election of officers in fall 1936, Machen was defeated in his bid to be re-elected as president. In his place, Harold S. Laird, pastor of Faith Independent Church in Wilmington, Delaware, was elected; the vice president was also an independent church pastor. Control of the board passed to those who emphasized *independent* missions as opposed to *Presbyterian* missions. Eventually, the Presbyterian Church of America would defund this missions board that had done so much to create the new denomination.

The final issue that would create friction in the new church was over Christian liberty, which was code for "whether or not Christians could drink alcoholic beverages in moderation." From the mid-nineteenth century on, "temperance" and eventually "total abstinence" from alcoholic beverage were marks of a consecrated believer. And for a time in the United States, it was illegal to produce and sell beverage alcohol, a position codified in the Eighteenth Amendment to the United States Constitution. Several ministers, led by J. Oliver Buswell, then president of Wheaton College, desired the church to go on record supporting total abstinence from alcoholic beverages.

Such a position was problematic for a couple of reasons. The first was that Machen had voted against similar provisions in the late 1910s. When the Eighteenth Amendment was being ratified, the New Brunswick Presbytery had a resolution that supported the government in this effort; Machen voted against this resolution, a fact that was used against him in the 1920s when he was being considered for the chair of Apologetics at Princeton Seminary. But the second problem was one that the Westminster Seminary faculty pointed out: total abstinence from alcohol seemed to reject Jesus' own example in turning water into wine and then having it served at the wedding feast of Cana. To bind people's consciences contrary to God's Word and Jesus' own example should not happen. Of course, there was a further irony here: those who were arguing for liberty on the church's teaching regarding last things were denying liberty to those who believed that the Bible allowed drinking of alcohol in moderation. It was a conflict that needed to find a resolution.

All three of these issues would combine to divide the church. Perhaps as a mercy to Machen, he would not be alive to see the division of the church that he had helped to birth. At the third General Assembly, which met in mid-

June 1937, a failure to elect their candidate for moderator caused a group of seventeen ministers headed by Carl McIntire and J. Oliver Buswell to leave and form the Bible Presbyterian Synod. However, the blow of the division of 1937 was more psychological than material. It seemed to portend that this "true Presbyterian Church" would find itself battling for its existence and sorting out what in the world Machen's vision meant for faithful life in this world.

9

A Father in Israel

Machen's workload and stress levels throughout mid-1930s had been significant and intense. Not only was he the main financial backer of Westminster Seminary, the Independent Board, and the *Presbyterian Guardian*, but also he was the face of the new institutions to most of evangelical Protestantism. While no one knew who Cornelius Van Til, John Murray, or Ned Stonehouse were in 1934, many conservative evangelicals knew Machen's name and ability. As a result, he was constantly writing, defending, and promoting these agencies.

One task that he took on as a way of promoting the work of Westminster Seminary was a weekly radio show. Starting in early 1935 and extending until his death two years later, Machen regularly appeared on WIP radio station in Philadelphia in order to give short talks on doctrinal topics. Most of these talks were published as *The Christian Faith in the Modern World* (1936) and *The Christian View of Man* (1937); he had hoped to publish two additional collections that would further treat doctrine on a popular level. In the first book, Machen unpacked a basic set of arguments concerning who God was and whether he had spoken: verbal plenary inspiration was defended; the character of God as Trinity was set forth; and the person and work of Jesus was detailed. Machen moved on in the second book to provide a biblical understanding of human beings: how they were created, how they participated in original sin, and how they might be saved. Taken as a pair, these two books deserve to be more well known.

At the time, these radio addresses were yet one more thing to do. He had just finished writing the addresses that would make up the third year of radio talks and had delivered five of them through December 1936. The talks centered on the doctrine of the atonement, the Christian belief that Jesus died on the cross as a substitute, satisfying God's wrath against his chosen ones and gaining righteousness from God to impute to his own. At one point, he summarized the teaching, "His death was the crown of His active obedience. It was the crown of that obedience to the law of God by which He merited eternal life

for those whom He came to save. Do you not see, then, what the true state of the case is? Christ's active obedience and His passive obedience are not two divisions of His work ... but every event of His life was both active obedience and passive obedience. Every event of His life was a part of His payment of the penalty of sin, and every event of His life was a part of that glorious keeping of the law of God by which He earned for His people the reward of eternal life. The two aspects of His work, in other words, are inextricably intertwined. Neither was performed apart from the other. Together they constitute the wonderful, full salvation which was wrought for us by Christ our Redeemer."

Shortly after giving this address, Machen boarded a plane for North Dakota, where he would preach in a number of churches and hold a rally for the new Presbyterian Church of America. He arrived in Bismarck, North Dakota, at the end of December; it was twenty degrees below zero. He went to preach in Carson and Leith; at the end of his preaching, he was struck with pleurisy. His host immediately got him to the car and drove him back, seventy-five miles, to Bismarck. After consulting a doctor, Machen refused hospitalization and kept his evening preaching engagement.

But the following day, when he wanted to leave for Philadelphia and home, the doctor refused to let him leave and forced him to go to the hospital. His condition worsened there as he was diagnosed with pneumonia. On Thursday, New Year's Eve, he was slipping in and out of consciousness; when he was conscious, his mind was active and sharp, but he was profoundly sick. The following day, Friday, New Year's Day, 1937, he dictated a final telegram, this one to his Westminster Seminary colleague John Murray, who had assisted him with his radio addresses: "I'm so thankful for active obedience of Christ. No hope without it." Shortly after sending this, he died at 7:30pm on January 1, 1937.

Machen's body returned to Philadelphia and a memorial service was held at Spruce Street Baptist Church on January 5. There was a graveside service later as his body was laid to rest in the family plot at Greenmount Cemetery in Baltimore, Maryland. But though Machen's friends and followers had said goodbye to him, they were still stunned that he was gone. He was only fifty-five years old, not noticeably in ill-health beyond a certain air of exhaustion and a surprising loss of weight that had occurred during the previous summer.

For Ned Stonehouse, Machen's colleague in teaching New Testament at Westminster Seminary as well as in editing the *Presbyterian Guardian*, the pain was obvious. "We have depended so much upon him in the past that it might well appear that we could not go on without him," Stonehouse wrote. Machen was Elijah to Stonehouse's Elisha, indeed, to countless others who looked to him as a spiritual father: "He was notably the spiritual father of a generation of theological students who crowded into his classrooms." But there was also friendship and natural affection; "to many of us he manifested all of the affection that a natural father might possibly bestow upon his sons." Here was a true loss—the loss of a father in Israel.

And this loss was just at the crucial time in the life of the new Presbyterian denomination that Machen had helped to birth. The second General Assembly of the Presbyterian Church of America had recessed just six weeks before Machen's death. That meeting had held the church together largely through the force of Machen's prestige and personality. With him now gone, others stepped in to fill the leadership gap. Stonehouse, as editor of the *Presbyterian Guardian*, along with fellow Westminster Seminary faculty members John Murray and Cornelius Van Til, stood on one side of the growing divide in the new church. On the other side, J. Oliver Buswell and Carl

McIntire took significant leadership roles in representing what they understood the new church to be.

Throughout the first six months of 1937, both sides worked to define what the new church would be. Murray and Stonehouse wrote significant essays in the *Presbyterian Guardian* attacking Buswell's premillennialism and his position on abstinence from alcohol. McIntire appeared at a faculty meeting of Westminster Seminary and urged them to stand for total abstinence from alcohol and to add faculty and trustees who held to premillennialism in order to achieve a certain balance in views. When both of these suggestions were rejected, Allan MacRae, professor of Old Testament at Westminster, resigned, as did two Westminster trustees (one of whom, ironically, was Harold S. Laird, the man who ousted Machen from the presidency of the Independent Board just a few months before). Having lost the seminary, the McIntire/Buswell group began plans to start a rival school for the fall, Faith Theological Seminary.

With the movement of the Independent Board toward independency and away from Presbyterianism along with the start of a rival seminary to Westminster, it was probably inevitable that the small Presbyterian Church of America would divide at the third General Assembly (which actually occurred a year after the church was founded). The first matter that came up was the report of the committee on Foreign Missions, which recommended that the church sever its relationship with the Independent Board and start its own denominational missions work. A minority report, presented by Carl McIntire, served to rehearse all the issues of division, especially the charge that a "little clique" centered at Westminster Seminary was attempting to run everything. However, the minority report was defeated soundly and the church agreed to start its own missions work.

This debate set the stage for the next and decisive issue, represented by three overtures on the issue of Christian liberty and total abstinence from alcohol. The three overtures boiled down to two basic positions: on the one side, a firm and vocal commitment to total abstinence in line with the affirmations of the New School Presbyterian General Assembly (1840) and the reunited PCUSA (1877); on the other side, an equally firm commitment simply to restate what the Westminster Standards said on liberty of conscience without advocating abstinence from alcohol. In the end, the latter position won the day by a large majority.

Immediately after this assembly ended, fourteen ministers and three elders—led by Carl McIntire and J. Oliver Buswell—withdrew from the Presbyterian Church of America and announced their intention to form the Bible Presbyterian Synod. In their first year, they would meet and affirm total abstinence, premillennialism and the Scofield Reference Bible, and the Independent Board for Presbyterian Foreign Missions. They would also claim the new Faith Seminary as their denominational seminary; and they would ordain their first new minister that year, a passionate young man who would eventually make his own mark, Francis Schaeffer.

By 1939, not only was Machen's already small church smaller, but also it was forced to give up its name. Sued by the PCUSA for having a name too close to its own, the church chose the name "the Orthodox Presbyterian Church" (OPC). And the 1940s would bring yet another secession from the group—once again, the underlying issues centered on whether or not the OPC saw itself as a conservative mainline church. When the OPC answered that question negatively, emphasizing confessional particularity over ecumenical engagement and evangelical promotion, several leaders left including Robert Strong, Gordon Clark, and Edwin Rian.

One of the questions that arose during that first decade was whether the church would have followed a different trajectory had Machen survived pneumonia. After all, by 1946, he would have only been sixty-five; his influence would have been, if possible, even more significant in the church and in emerging postwar evangelicalism. Would he have steered the church toward an engagement with this evangelicalism and away from the isolationism that became the OPC's keynote during the late 1940s and 1950s?

Some believe that he would not have engaged evangelicals. Historians D. G. Hart and John Muether, for example, note, "Had Machen lived, perhaps he could have provided the stability and leadership necessary to find a compromise. His own activities in the church controversies of the 1930s, however, reveal that compromise would have been difficult ... From its inception the OPC was faced with a choice between being Reformed and being fundamentalist. From Machen's perspective there was never any doubt about what the church should be ... As it turned out, the Reformed identity of the OPC after the division of 1937 was virtually identical to Machen's original vision for the church."

Perhaps, but then again, perhaps not: after all, Machen had shown a reflexive evangelicalism throughout the

1920s and early 1930s, speaking to a wide range of groups in an effort to battle against modernism and defend the biblical faith. And while he most certainly stood for Presbyterianism, he also was more than willing to go outside the regular pathways of Presbyterian polity in order to create new institutions (Westminster Seminary; Independent Board; the OPC) or to do new types of outreach (radio ministry).

Further, it is hard to know exactly how Machen would have responded to the opportunities of the rising evangelicalism of the 1940s. With the dominance of liberal thought at Union Seminary in New York City in the 1930s and 1940s along with the rise of neo-orthodoxy at Princeton Seminary during the same period, the dividing lines between orthodoxy and heterodoxy became even more clear during this period. Even if Machen had held the young church together, would they have received more interest in those days? Likewise, the new energy of postwar evangelicalism—represented by Billy Graham and Harold Ockenga (a Westminster Seminary graduate)—coupled with the young intellectual leaders who had trained at Westminster Seminary—such as future Fuller Seminary faculty members E. J. Carnell and Paul K. Jewett— might have drawn a Machen-led OPC closer to the new evangelical orbit. If the "father in Israel" had survived, the OPC might not have become as separatist as it became.

That said, Machen probably would not have found much encouragement in the new social conscience of postwar evangelicals, signaled by Carl F. H. Henry's *The Uneasy Conscience of Modern Fundamentalism* (1947). After all, Machen had a clear sense that one could not "expect from a true Christian church any official pronouncements upon the political or social questions of the day." The idea that any church—and especially a Presbyterian church—would become "a political lobby, through the advocacy of political measures whether good or bad" was an anathema. The activism of postwar American evangelicals would probably have made Machen extremely nervous.

In addition, while recognizing that evangelicalism was a broad coalition that stood against modernism and for the gospel, Machen would also have been nervous about postwar evangelicals' *de facto* assumption that dispensationalism was the only faithful way of reading Scripture. That would have been different from the situation that Machen faced in the 1920s; however, the ascendant influence of Dallas Theological Seminary, which started in the 1920s, would have made dispensationalism a more significant issue for a postwar Machen.

In the event, Machen's death in 1937 made all of these speculations moot. Still, the influence that Machen has continued to extend over the seventy-five years since his death is remarkable. Not only has his classic book, *Christianity and Liberalism*, remained in print since he first wrote it in 1923, but his Greek language primer continues in print as well. His seminary trained the first generation of evangelical scholars and spawned a generation of churchmen, not only for the OPC, but for the southern Presbyterian church and its successor denomination, the Presbyterian Church in America. Westminster Seminary served as the model (and competitor) both for Fuller Seminary when it was founded in 1947 and for Gordon-Conwell Theological Seminary when it was created through a merger in 1969. Significantly, both newer theological schools were led by

Ockenga, who never got beyond his training at Princeton and Westminster Seminaries and the influence of Machen.

Even in the work of Carl F. H. Henry and Francis Schaeffer, the Machen legacy made a significant impact on American evangelicalism. Henry helped to revive evangelical interest in engaging with the best academic training and thought; Schaeffer, who trained at Westminster Seminary before transferring to and graduating from McIntire's Faith Seminary, employed many of the same apologetic approaches that Machen had used in his 1935–36 radio addresses. And to be sure, the impact of that original Westminster Seminary faculty itself is impossible to gauge. In John Murray, Cornelius Van Til, Ned Stonehouse, and E. J. Young, the faculty had four leading scholars whose publications served to anchor mid-century evangelicals in biblical truth. Most of their writings likewise continue in print, furthering the Machen legacy to the present day.

For all of these evangelicals and confessional Presbyterians, Machen was truly a father in Israel. Yet for those who do not share his faith and who remember him at all, he will always be remembered as a fundamentalist and, what is more, a fundamentalist on the losing side of history. And so, in that regard, it is helpful to come back to the journalist H. L. Mencken and his evaluation of Machen.

In his obituary for Machen, Mencken noted that most journalists and their readers failed to understand Machen correctly. "The generality of readers, I suppose, gathered thereby the notion that he was simply another Fundamentalist on the order of William Jennings Bryan and the simian faithful of Appalachia," Mencken observed.

"But he was actually a man of great learning, and, what is more, of sharp intelligence."

What caused Mencken to respect Machen even while he disagreed with him was that Machen refused to compromise the fundamentals of the Christian faith and the Presbyterian form of that belief. Machen "fell out with the reformers who have been trying, in late years, to convert the Presbyterian Church into a kind of literary and social club, devoted vaguely to good works." Though he failed to prevent the liberal reformers from doing this, Mencken knew that Machen understood that religion was "far more deep-down-diving and mud-upbringing" than liberals confessed. "Dr. Machen tried to impress that obvious fact upon his fellow adherents of the Genevan Mohammed. He failed—but he was undoubtedly right."

And perhaps this is Machen's most important legacy. Not simply as a fundamentalist or a confessionalist, an evangelical or a Presbyterian—but as a Christian, as a defender of biblical orthodoxy, as an apologist for the gospel. To be sure, he was a father in Israel for those he left behind in his just-birthed institutions; and he was "Doctor Fundamentalis" to Mencken and the intelligentsia. But for the rest of us, Machen was a historical Mr. Valiant-for-Truth from John Bunyan's *Pilgrim's Progress*. When the merry band on their way to the Celestial City came across Mr. Valiant-for-Truth, they saw him use his sword, a true Jerusalem blade. And as he described his battles, he noted, "I fought till my sword did cleave to my hand; and then they were joined together as if a sword grew out of my arm; and when the blood ran through my fingers, then I fought with most courage." Indeed, Machen did, Mr. Valiant-for-Truth, one faithful unto death, courageous to the end.

For Further Reading

BOOKS BY MACHEN

D. G. Hart, ed., *J. Gresham Machen: Selected Shorter Writings* (Phillipsburg, NJ: P&R, 2004).

J. Gresham Machen, *A Christian View of Man* ([1937] Carlisle: Banner of Truth, 1995).

_____, *Christianity and Liberalism*, new edition ([1923] Grand Rapids: Eerdmans, 2009).

_____, *God Transcendent*, ed. Ned B. Stonehouse ([1949] Carlisle: Banner of Truth, 1982).

_____, *What is Faith?* ([1925] Carlisle: Banner of Truth, 1991);

_____, *Virgin Birth of Christ* ([1930] London: James Clarke, 1958),

Barry Waugh, ed., *Letters from the Front: J. Gresham Machen's Correspondence from World War I* (Phillipsburg, NJ: P&R, 2012)

BOOKS ABOUT MACHEN

D. G. Hart, *Defending the Faith: J. Gresham Machen and the Crisis of Conservative Protestantism in Modern America* (Baltimore: Johns Hopkins University Press, 1994).

Bradley J. Longfield, *The Presbyterian Controversy: Fundamentalists, Modernists, and Moderates* (New York: Oxford University Press, 1991).

Stephen J. Nichols, *J. Gresham Machen: A Guided Tour of his Life and Thought* (Phillipsburg, NJ: P&R, 2004).

Ned B. Stonehouse, *J. Gresham Machen: A Biographical Memoir* ([1954] Carlisle: Banner of Truth, 1987).